Copyright © 2023 – FyeN Publishing Services a division of Fye Network

All rights to this book are reserved. No permission is given for any part of this book to be reproduced, transmitted in any form or means; electronic or mechanical, stored in a retrieval system, photocopied, recorded, scanned, or otherwise. Any of these actions require the proper written permission of the author.

Author: Ismail Badjie

Book Cover and Designer: Mariana Ostanik

Cover photo by: Lucas Gouvêa (Unsplash)

Editor: Sulayman Njie, Ph.D.

DISCLAIMER

The exceptions to the preceding are short quotations within other publications and short passages by the media only with the included references of title, author, and publisher.

For more information about custom editions, special sales and premium and corporate purchases please contact Fyen Publishing Services at publishing@fyenetwork.com

Visit us on the web!

www.fyenetwork.com

Printed by IngramSpark

Printed in the United States of America

First Printing Edition, 2023

ISBN: 978-0-9993307-7-7

Table of Contents

Letters to my daughter: Dear Isha Haddy
    Chapter 1: Love In Spite Of (Part I) 09
    Chapter 2: Love In Spite Of (Part II) 16
    Chapter 3: Spiritually In You 21
    Chapter 4: Curse Of Ambition 32

Call me Ismaila (I am Gambian):
    Chapter 5: Highly Schooled And Uneducated 37
    Chapter 6: Reimagining Nationality 46
    Chapter 7: Country Of Indifference 52
    Chapter 8: Exemplary Youth 58

An exercise on vulnerability:
    Chapter 9: Preying Monsters With Beads 64
    Chapter 10: What's Love Got To Do With It? 69
    Chapter 11: Ps I Love You, Man 76
    Chapter 12: My True North 81

Call me Ishmail (I am American):
    Chapter 13: Hello Cousin 89
    Chapter 14: That Body, That Body 96
    Chapter 15: God, Please Sit This One Out 101
    Chapter 16: The Immigrant Grief That Was MAGA 107

Finding Ismail (On Trials, tribulations, and new beginnings):
    Chapter 17: Brave, Afraid And Alive..120

    Chapter 18: Heart, Nerve And Sinew, Please Hold On........................128

    Chapter 19 : The Wax Between Two Lit Ends.......................................138

E Pluribus Unum: Out of many, one
    Chapter 20: Life As A Hyphen..144

Preface

The process of creating the pieces in this book has been fueled by moments of introspection, a multitude of questions about life, and moments of deep uncertainty and vulnerability. In my late 20s, I discovered that writing was not only a creative outlet but also a cathartic and therapeutic release for the many thoughts that consumed me. The purpose of my writing is not to provide answers, condemn social constructs that I am a product of, or establish unwavering opinions. Instead, it is to document my observations and offer a profound learning opportunity for readers from all backgrounds who are curious about the diverse intricacies of individuals of African origin.

To my beloved daughter, Isha Haddy, I dedicate this book to you. As I matured, I realized the importance of understanding my parents' experiences, which had a profound impact on shaping them into human beings tasked with raising 5 children. Your birth inspired me to document my life in real-time, giving you the opportunity to understand my story through my own lens. I hope it provides guidance for when you embark on your journey of self-exploration and self-actualization. Isha you will always be my true north and muse. I hope you grow to realize that there is strength in vulnerability, to always choose courage over comfort, and to trust your sensibilities as an African woman.

My mercurial nature has made being my wife, father, mother, sister, brother, and friend only sustainable through enduring love, patience, and acceptance. To Yeya (Haddy), Papa (Dembo), Adama (Na Fula Musso Musu Nyimaa), Malick (Sas), Fatim (Fine), Isatou (Isha B) and Ebrima (E-boy). Thank you.
I am eternally grateful for the circle of loved ones especially during my entrepreneurial journey, which has been filled with immense uncertainty. My family and close friends will always be the anchor and I love each and every one of them dearly. I hope through this piece of work, and the peeling of the layers of my idiosyncrasies will reveal moments of clarity and deeper understanding of me.

To my readers, I hope this book provides confirmation that life is full of questions, fears, doubts, and opportunities to unpack childhood experiences and take bold strides towards becoming better versions of ourselves. Navigating the social agreements around elusive concepts such as our cultural identities, nationalities and modes of spirituality can be challenging in the 21st century but I truly believe we as humans have more experiences and aspirations in common than we do differences.

Last but not least, I want to sincerely thank the entire Fyen Publishing Team and editor Dr. Saul Njie for helping bring this project to fruition.

Enjoy the roller coaster, and I hope it invokes similar introspection and meaningful conversations with the people you love.

Letters to my daughter: Dear Isha Haddy

CHAPTER ONE

LOVE, IN SPITE OF... (PART I)

(Written September 2018)

A letter to my daughter.

    I remember the first day the ultrasound doppler hovered over your peanut sized being. Your heart beating to the rhythm of a tamma (Senegambian drum) as a spiritual confirmation of the miracle that you indeed were. Lost for words at that moment, the tears rolling down your mother's face were symbolic of a part of ourselves that was no more. Trails of two selfish beings cleansed by our own love creation. As the days and months went by, I marveled at how each moment ushered a significant growth milestone in your being. The walls of your heart forming, brain cells firing up, veins and arteries growing into viable channels of life, with each genesis and permutation of organ development presenting a delicate opportunity for something to go wrong.

A pair of X chromosomes from your mother and I respectively undergoing a sequence of life generation that will make you in essence, us. Something in me also felt different every time we heard the "beating of the drum." Almost a re-awakening of my heart to experience true purity in love. A serene transformation from always choosing what to love to being presented with a being I am bound to love hard, unconditionally.

A bewildering confession I have however is that I had only formed one vivid projection of what you will become. The audacity I had to just conceptualize life with a boy was beyond the required appreciation for the gift of a healthy child growing in your mother's womb. Not only are my seeds responsible for the 'Y' *(chromosome)* in such a creation, the burden of nurturing such a delicate process lies entirely on your mother, who was void of a "Y." How could I have such a profound subconscious yet selfish trait common in many aspiring fathers I knew and talked to. A victim of my unconscious patriarchal bias despite all the phenomenal women I have been blessed to know in your grandmother *(Haddy)* and aunts *(Fatim and Isha)*.

Was hoping for a boy an admission of men's perceived emotional inability to commit to loving and caring for a woman who was not our mother unconditionally? A sense of an anticipatory burden knowing being emotionally available and present in a woman's life was a requirement for their emotional fortitude. Did it stem from a guilty conscience knowing our predatory track record with females? Or was it merely rooted in the history of our species where fathers saw sons as infant comrades not requiring delicate attention and manufacturing of their emotional warehouses? I wonder if awareness of our inherent shortcomings creates an expected cognitive convergence in boys as they grow up to see the same intrinsic flaws manifest in themselves. "Be strong!", "Men don't cry!", "Girls love Alpha men!", "You are a King destined for greatness!" all battered into a young boy's mind to create a cloak of aspirational indifference to any shortcoming being a barrier to delivering their father's legacy project. A definite expression of love indeed but one that calls for better understanding.

Our societies and families enable such legacy projects despite a mountain of evidence to the contrary. Women in today's society, when given equal access to proper opportunities, prove to be a surer bet for success than men. This fact is even more profound in our homeland of The Gambia where us men are raised with such little requirements of fortitude and independence that a new generation of educated and accomplished women are left wondering where "Able and Stable Samba Banjul" is (Who is not 20 years older!). It's the myth of the Lion King. Stories framed around the son who grew up to become king under an established patriarchal line of succession irrespective of the presence of any woman in the family of surer virtues fit to rule.

Every shortcoming or flaw present in a father becomes a virtue he seeks to correct and see manifest in his son, a surrogate form of redemption. A son that becomes a better ruler than he was, finally makes it to the league and play professional sports or eventually attain a doctorate degree and bear the initials in front of the family name. All efforts to fulfill not a son's self-manifested desire but the legacy of the father. The irony behind such a preference is the stronger affinity boys tend to have not for their fathers, but for their mothers. The mothers expose them to the virtues of love from birth and shape every other form of love they seek through adulthood. Additionally, the same primal "divide and conquer" instincts present in fathers manifest in most sons evolving into rivals in masculine prowess chasing their own legacy projects as the once strong and dominant fathers wither away from old age. The special bond between a father and his daughter tends to be rooted in a brand of unconditional love men initially undervalue and therefore always presents itself as "the gift" and "good luck" your grandfather and uncle speak about.

I am aware that the brand of love from me to you will undoubtedly shape yours for the rest of your life. Similar to most men, I have come to realize that I have benefitted from a sense of privilege when it comes to Love . I have always been granted the right to "Love, because of……." and never succumb to the condition of "Loving, in spite of." A psychological sense of entitlement reinforced throughout the lives of men is our right to choose who we love under certain conditions while girls are raised to present themselves in a way they can be "chosen."

Throughout human civilization, such a privilege has been reinforced and indoctrinated into social ecosystems and languages across all cultures. When Love is spoken of concerning men and women, privilege always lies within the man's choice. A level of tolerance of all levels of imperfection with hopes of still being Loved, in spite of. It's one of the few privileges that transcends race, religion, and culture. Our whole idea of romance stems from the premise of a woman presenting herself to be chosen by a man she may also deem desirable. The dynamic is such that the man may Love her because she is beautiful, because she is kind, because she is educated and wealthy, because she is (insert any superlative) with full recognition of his flaws but with a defiant expectation of the reciprocity coming with a brand of unconditional Love, in spite of. The slightest deviation in the love he receives re-activates his sense of privilege and entitlement to make the "choice" to migrate that Love to another woman because of (insert any dissatisfaction). As a woman you are therefore forced to accept double standards of love, sex and relationships all in efforts to not jeopardize "prince charming" riding on a white horse to return your glass slipper.

I have heard sayings such as *"Goor du nyaww"* (A man cannot be ugly/unattractive) from some of your grandmothers growing up thinking it was the true manifestation of said privilege. A form of leverage shown in a woman's expectation to still Love in spite of any physical or nonphysical shortcoming a man had because it provided a level of security being "chosen" has provided. Such idioms are not only embedded in the Wolof language, and African culture as a whole but has also manifested in the social engineering of how boys approached love in such a transactional manner. It creates an unbalanced expectation that exposes them to devastating blows of heartbreak when the privilege of choosing who they love is stripped away by a woman who chooses not to love them in spite of their shortcomings.

The intricacies of all these dynamics of love have left me puzzled and scared about how your first love (Me) will shape your resistance or submission to such privilege. I wonder if, by God's creation alone, you are even capable of not Loving in spite of. I believe it is the purest form of love that creates the fortitude all women require to withstand the mental, physical, and emotional toll it takes to give life to a child, care and nurture it into adulthood.

The anticipation of meeting you has me trying to process and understand this new form of love I have never experienced. I feel like I owe it to you to tell you so much about life and how the variations of love received and given have shaped me into the flawed yet hopeful being I am today. My love for you will develop the brand you seek but will be elusive to replicate as you evolve into a woman and run into so many variations that may vye for your attention. How can I prevent your first heartbreak? How can I love you so hard it renders you not easily impressed with or desperately crave the love and attention of a man unworthy of you? How can I delay the numerous times a man you care deeply about falls victim to his selfish ways and disappoints you or betrays your trust. Would I be that man at some point yet expect your love, in spite of? Should I even want to protect you from love encounters with men that will build your emotional muscle and acumen to decipher their true intentions? But how could I not protect you? Thoughts of a man breaking your heart alone induce rage potent enough to have intentions of grabbing my Ruger and inflicting insurmountable physical pain on said man. But would casting such an umbrella of protection not mask the very cynicism and fickle nature of love I know you will learn to see?

As you grow older, I hope you will see enough in my steadfast love for you as one that evolved because of you, in spite of many attempts by other women to harness such potency. I would warn you against men like me who will make efforts at "choosing" you because of your virtues and not in spite of any of your perceived imperfections. Men like me who have had the privilege of being selfish in seeking a love that is conducive to their desires. Men like me who will take your love for granted because its manifestation is one, they will not be mature enough to see a lifetime of value in. Men like me who succumb to a relentless pursuit of achieving "success" in the world. Giving their absolute best to all powers that be leaving behind an attention-depleted rest of themselves to nurture relationships that will undoubtedly be the only success worth seeking to be happy.

Hopefully, in the love between us, you have a vacuum in your need for a brand of love and validation that makes you lower the threshold of your "in spite of" just to be "Chosen" by an unworthy man. Embody a sense of value and self-worth so high, the superlatives that make men love you "because of" place all the power of choice right in your hands. I pray you deem all societal norms surrounding love irrelevant and prevent them from infiltrating your mind. Use the familiarity of love from us your parents and family as a layer of vibranium over you as you grow up to become a manifested woman.

I look forward to holding you in my arms and watching you blossom from my little princess to the queen you will become insha'Allah. There's a beauty in the vulnerability I feel as I anticipate a lifelong journey with you filled with an abundant supply of love, comfort, friendship, and security. You are and will always be my muse. My reason why.

One thing is for sure when it comes to Love and Choice; I am glad God chose an angel in you, for me; In spite of......

Love,

Not DR. IDB... just Daddy

She who lives....

September 22nd, 2018: 4:15pm

I never knew falling in love, at first sight, could be so powerful. The emotions I feel are simply indescribable. I used to think I was stronger than average until I saw your mother endure the long hours of labor to bring you into this world. A woman's mettle is truly divine, and a gift of life is something I can never reciprocate through material things. Witnessing your birth was a spiritual out of body experience that has left me humbled and in awe of your mother's endurance and selflessness. Do not ever take her love and sacrifice for granted.

I thank God for your mother, and we love you so much.

Always and forever our little princess

You are simply perfect.

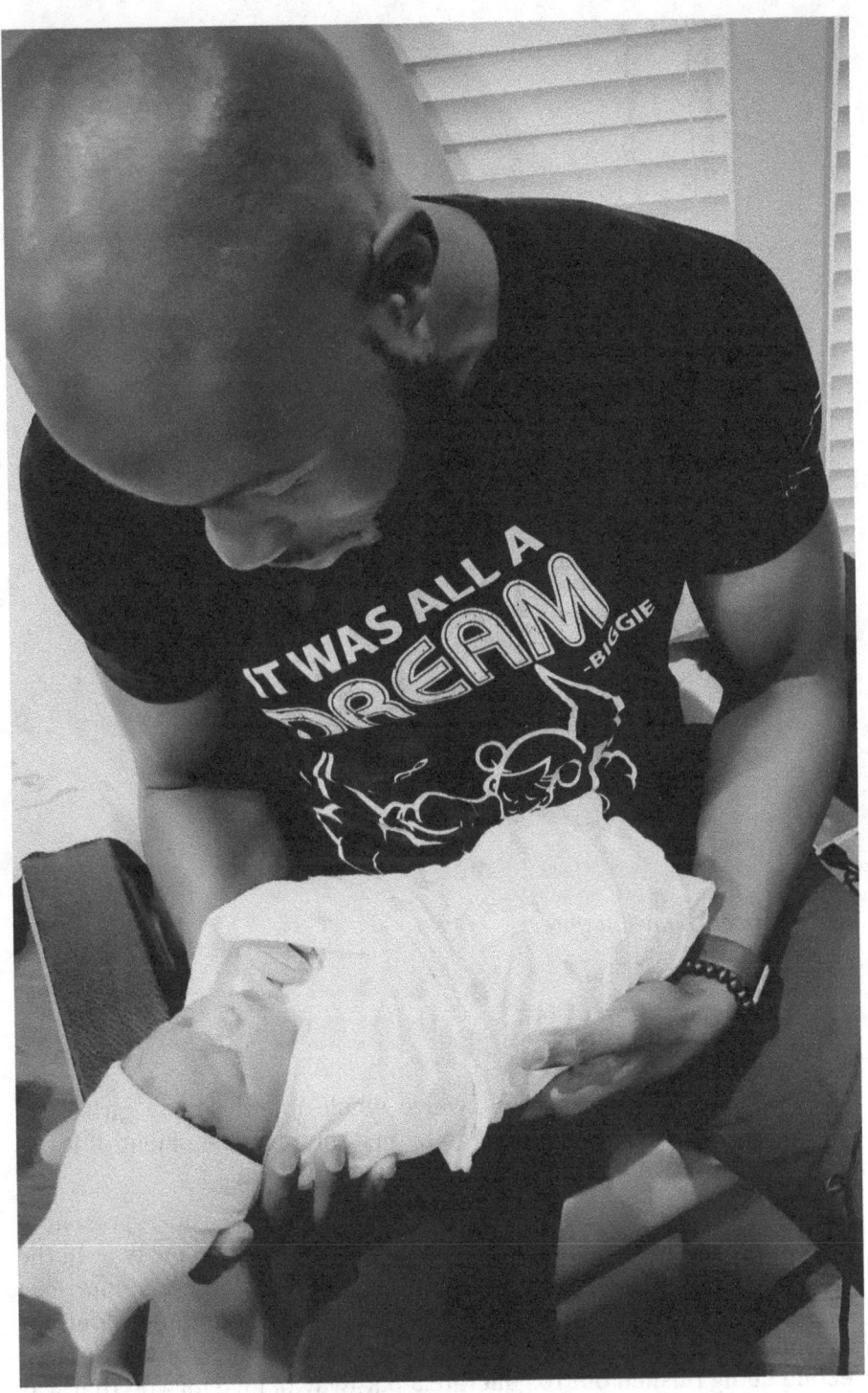
My first moments with Isha (Mbanyako) after her birth. Pure love at first sight.

CHAPTER TWO

LOVE IN SPITE OF (PART II)

(Written October 2019)

A Letter to my daughter...

A redemptive kind of love

I cannot believe it's been twelve whole months baby girl! They warned me that the days would go by fast, but every moment of it has been an infusion of joy that I could not have imagined.

I wrote to and about you earlier partly because you represented seeds of new life and a new type of love God was sending my way. In the deepest layers of vulnerability lay a juxtaposition of knowing our love was going to challenge me to love in ways I have resisted for a lifetime. My emotional detachment to always needing assurance of love and affection being flushed out to generate a pathway of love for you that was continually streaming with abundance.

Sometimes it feels like our emotional channel is way too familiar and sophisticated for your small being. A bond that always forces me to be emotionally honest and being receptive to your love at all times, non-negotiable. It's in the way you hold back your smile until my attention is undivided and eyes locked into your heart-melting gaze. In the way you conduct an emotional scan when I come home. Poking parts of my face as if you can read all frequencies of the world's burdens placed on your dad before embracing me. It's in the way you scream "da-da" to get my attention from afar to announce or dramatically display new layers of your jovial foolery. These moments give me life, Isha. Love that feels safe and pure. A true re-awakening of my senses packaged as this delicate gift of ours.

I know this potent but redemptive kind of love between us screams confirmations of me never opening my heart to love wholeheartedly. The anti *"risk it all"* type of love that I used as emotional armor to protect me from heartbreak. It was effective but always felt like a straight jacket depriving my lungs an ability to simply…breathe and welcome a warm embrace of mutual love.

The idea of depending on confirmation of love from someone else to thrive emotionally was always a predisposition foreign to me until you came into my life. So 33 years of what should have been a deep understanding of love as we see and express it was delayed and its code locked until I was given a chance to love you, in spite of

An unmatched kind of love. No person will and can ever match the amount of love I have for you baby. So I think it's essential for you to grow up knowing that all the love you will ever need will be right here to fill you. I know my current logic may be flawed and rooted in my very own avoidance, but It's my surest bet for protecting you from a world of hurt love can bring along. As humans, the swinging pendulum of our emotional affinity to be loved can go from a healthy one that works in a complementary fashion to a toxic one that reeks of dependency and abuse.

You can be a loving person who cares deeply for individuals who add emotional value to your life, but people have a natural proclivity to disappoint you irrespective of their profession of love for you. The intensity of the disappointment, however, always lies in your calibrated expectations. Only a full bucket can overflow into another; therefore, expecting love to flow in a bidirectional way when one party barely loves themselves enough will always be a taxing exercise in futility.

One thing I will also admit to you is that even though your mother can never love you "more" than I do, I can never match her level of care and attention even if I tried. Watching the two of you has shown me layers of potency in an unrelenting kind of love and care that God only truly transfixed in women. It's juggling the a.m. routines to feed and clothe you, the 45 hour work weeks for her to come home and still have you demand her clocking into your needs that simply display her superhero strengths. Your love is her rocket fuel so don't you ever take her for granted without reciprocating it.

I watch the two of you from afar and notice the subtleties in your own very expressions of emotions. You're intuitive enough to know when hunger strikes, there's nothing daddy's chest can provide you to suckle yourself to comfort. While at the same time, knowing exactly when to use my soft heart and tender reception to your demands after failed attempts with your mother. It's a beautiful experience to watch and in her (your mother), true admiration for her selflessness when it comes to your love and security. I hope you grow up to fully appreciate the power of a woman's love, especially one from your mother. A magical power you will also possess one day, so do not be fooled for a second that love from a man could ever match that.

Watching the bond the two of you have always made me see the constant conflation we have with how we throw around the word "Love" as casually as we do. Love from your parents is anchored in a commitment. A *"you gotta eat but we want to sleep...so to hell with our sleep"* kind of commitment. Romantic love, on the other hand, is rooted in well ....dopamine and unrealistic expectations. Men will always send alerts to your brain about this great romance that is upon you, but the burning desire never lasts as long nor does it remain as consistent and unconditional . So, be aware of the difference as you navigate the world.

The paradox of my love

As I reflect on the past 12 months of your life, our life, I can't help but feel the weight of how choices I have made affect you. A "curse of my ambition" is perhaps one way of describing it. You came into this world when I was at a *crossroads* desperately seeking deliverance to a new purpose and passion, knowing it was going to come at a steep price. It kept me away too many nights when my desperation to nurture this other baby I have, stole me away from you. It's a painful paradox of knowing what I love the most in this world inspired me to embark on a journey that inadvertently robbed me of so many moments with you. Moreover, God's sense of brutal humor seems to always expedite the growth in your physical and emotional expressions every time I am away.

I hope that one day when you grow older, you will understand, but no level of empathy can make up for my guilt. I miss you so much when I am on the road; I get nervous upon my return. Feelings of insecurity flooding my bloodstream like a teenage boy hoping she circles "yes" on a love proposition note. *"Would she remember the texture of my beard on her face—the warmth of my beating bare chest on her cheek?"*, *"how soon would she run to me with a warm embrace?"*, *would she cast that smile immediately upon sight?"* *"what if she starts speaking but doesn't say I love you too, daddy?"* because daddy has not been around. *"Would she still love in spite of all her father's shortcomings"* are all thoughts that continuously haunt me.

This very paradox of love perhaps your mother can never relate to because her selfless nature can never see worldly pursuits of legacy projects as contestable to being there for you. Therefore, this journey has been equally challenging for her knowing neither one of you signed up for such levels of discomfort in a nurturing process designed to be of two coequal parts. It keeps me up at night, knowing failure on this mission is not an option considering the sacrifices made. It also makes me wonder *(which I'm sure your mother does too)* what life would be like if I was merely content with living this "perfect family" life of two parents with stable jobs, a white picket fence, you and a dog running in the yard. But daddy isn't that guy. That picture always echoed a slow death from a life of monotony and comfort.

The very ambition and courageous moves the world may applaud will always place a veil over layers of our human experience it attenuates. The look on your face the plenty of times we've reunited in the past 12 months either from working shifts that spared but few intimate moments with you, or being across the world always spoke a thousand words. The clinching of your arms around my neck confirms you missed me while the penetrating gaze into my weary eyes acknowledged my current plight. If you could articulate words to ask *"how does it feel daddy?"*, I would sigh and tell you, "Heavy, baby…. Heavy".

The type of heavy I know won't kill me because God never places a burden too heavy to carry. Just heavy like the one that keeps a grit beneath the neutrality of my face through the days and nights navigating an arduous world. A mean *grit* like Dean big brother *"Untouchable"* told daddy will help keep his head *"bloody but unbowed"* even in *"the fell clutch of circumstance."* The tightening and curling of my chin and lips that prevent me from crying in some moments being the same group of facial muscles that keep me from bursting out in laughter.

I joke around with your mother saying I wish you never remember the time daddy quit his job and bet everything he ever owned on this one dream of his but also hope it serves as lessons for you to internalize and use as power. As men, I believe our ability to love is deeply tied to pursuing a life of fulfillment normally measured by our ability to earn and provide for the ones we love. Romantically, we easily surf the gray waves of lust and dissipating infatuation that can easily send the wrong signals. We can seek inspiration from the women in our lives, but the fundamental core remains in our love of self first before anything else.

This sobering reality is, even more, the case if it is not the version of imperfect but unrelenting love I have for you. Hence, when you start falling for your "Mr. Perfect" who will undoubtedly be shaped by how daddy was to you, please proceed with caution and recognize the price to pay that comes with men of great ambition. I pray that you utilize all the imperfections in how I give and receive love as navigation tools for you to love yourself so much that a man can only bring a complimentary "cup of love" to a chalice (yours) that is already overflowing with unconditional love. Your value and worth as a woman will always be tied to a man knowing access to your love and presence is a privilege that can be stripped away at any point because you don't depend on him to thrive.

At the end of the day, as long as the temerity of my now leads to a tomorrow for you that is void of instability and full of options in life to pursue, it would be worth the discomfort to me. Use my plight as an example to never allow anyone (including us) to cast boundaries around your wildest dreams and aspirations. Always choose courage over comfort. Find a way to lose yourself in the service of others for you owe it to humanity to leave the world in a slightly better place than you found it.

You will always be my muse and guiding light. Your happiness and security my true north.

If the joy of our love the past year is a sign of what's to come, you will forever be the beautiful gift of creation my heart yearned for.

Happy first birthday to my Isha Berry, my Isha Linguere, my Mbanyako....

Thank you for your love, in spite of...

Daddy has to go now, but your gentle spirit is now the armor I walk around with.

I Love you wholeheartedly

Da-dah

CHAPTER THREE

SPIRITUALLY IN YOU

(Written March 2020)

" Isha's first photoshoot" "God's greatest gift at 1 year old"

Gravity got the best of a teardrop streaming down my smiling face as I watched a video of you reading letters off a black hoodie your mother had on that read "BE THE DREAM". All I could mutter was *"Oh My God"* as I marveled at the sight of a child, my child, having the intellectual capacity unexpected at the tender age of 18 months where mere babbling of words was considered effective communication.

"Mashallah...We might have created a genius!" I muttered to your mother while pondering how much of the *"WE"* I contribute to. My DNA *(Nature)* indeed runs in your blood but your months on this earth have painfully been filled with my fleeting presence. Swinging back and forth into your life in flashes of pseudo-downtime and FaceTime calls like a shiny silver pendulum. Your mother and daycare teacher have always communicated with you as a mature and able being even if they realized your capacity was going to be a gradual process of leveling up *(Nurture)*. And leveling up fast you are doing! The experience, however, still feels like a spiritual manifestation of an extension of me. How your mannerisms and curiosity mirror me as a child. How the layers of your emotional depth and facial expressions mirror that of your mothers. Mechanisms of

a presentation I am unable to articulate but am fully convinced that our *(your parents)* spirits permeate in you.

God has already started stroking his paintbrush to highlight the hues and contours that will be your life's capacity using our blood as paint and our DNA as a blank canvas.

Although all those things may, in fact, be true, I still have no way of validating its veracity. Especially in contrast to your innate curiosity bundled with the effects availability of knowledge, information and ....older people around you have had on firing certain neurons in your brain faster than the average 18-month-old.

This conscious grappling with the things we cannot explain is a significant element of our foundation of spirituality my child. This safety net of attribution encapsulates our sanity in a way that provides a default answer to the unexplainable ..."*But GOD*"

Oh, Mama Africa

Isha Haddy, spirituality is a concept you will have your share of grappling with trying to understand how it is so much of who we are as hu mans, as African people. Having an unrelenting belief in a source of power we cannot see that elicits the most palpable vibrations of confirmation in our soul

I struggle with knowing when the right time in your life will be to have an honest conversation about religion and spirituality from an African context without breeding any doubt or cynicism in your heart. Should I allow your sponge-like reception and innocence to absorb the word of God through the lens of Islam until a robust moral foundation is built to withstand this weary world we live in? Or should I begin with your African heritage concerning the spirituality that you undoubtedly inherit?

As an African, the modern religions of Christianity and Islam have a dichotomous history on the continent that will evoke a spectrum of emotions in you as it does in me as adult. Setting the spiritual catalyst to build an individual relationship with God aside, elements of the religions will continuously remind you of a level of imperialism that was imposed on your African brethren. How could we have been the cradle of civilization and spirituality yet need outsiders who came to our lands to access our resources via trade, teach us about God and render our versions of spiritual expression primitive and unbecoming?

You will look through the annals of history and realize leaders of the Christian and Islamic faiths will one day have to answer for their indifference and endorsement of the mistreatment and religious brainwashing of the black man during the period of slavery when scriptures themselves were used to justify such a dehumanizing act. Africans were deemed uncivilized heathens whose souls were in dire need of salvation. Infused in their minds was a visual representation of a lord and savior to worship in spite of all their destitute and suffering on earth. Dangled in front of them was a promise of heaven in the hereafter while their masters built a utopia here on earth off their blood, sweat, and trail of tears. They stripped them from their lands, demolished their family structures and taught them about God from a manipulative oral interpretation of scriptures the Africans could neither read nor write. Slave owners tapped into the very innate spirituality they knew Africans possessed, transforming the white or Arab man as the vehicle of all things divine in the spiritual subconscious of their minds. (Sigh...)

The recognition of these historical facts is extremely uncomfortable (and heavy) to talk about and digest but undoubtedly necessary in the reconciliation of your identity as an African and the version of Islam you will be born into. I pray it never sows seeds of doubt in the presence/power of the Almighty or hatred and resentment towards any group of people. I pray it stimulates a better understanding of religion, spirituality and its purpose. Religion has always been a double-edged sword. Mankind has used it to spread tremendous love, kindness, and goodwill in the world while others use it regularly to infect hearts and minds spewing violence, hatred, and intolerance.

It feels like certain spirits only roam around within the borders of the motherland because our continent's spiritual allure seems to only appear in my consciousness when I return home to Africa. It's in everything we do. The constant reminders of giving out charity to seek blessings and drive away evildoers, the strict adherence to seeking prayer from masters of duality between the mythical arts and the religion of Islam down to the very economic impact it has on individuals spending the little resources they have on a "special" marabout man in hopes of delivering a promise.

Quite a perplexing recession-proof enterprise in an impoverished nation that produces cycles of mirages that confine individuals to sustaining the lives of marabout men with little investment in introspective analysis and addressing of self-limiting factors. If God is all-knowing with unlimited power to bless at will, how could a man be assigned keys to unlock the potential of his fellow man? It's almost akin to a bird seek reverence from a fellow bird to bless it with the ability to fly when God had its wings designed and attached from birth.

It is a striking contradiction I struggle to understand as much as I sometimes do feel the power of its existence. Living outside the confines of this mythical bubble has had a tendency to incite the most logical and pragmatic chambers of my brain. This is always in stark contrast to how our people consume their brand of spirituality. A level of unhealthy consumption that teeters on the edge of willful ignorance sprinkled with an unrelenting affinity to selective adherence. It's as if we believe so much in external forces of influences that we mortgage away any liability of self in the equation. This level of fear and adherence are aspects I hope you never give credence to. I have a decent level of curiosity, respect, and admiration for the secrets of African mythology but also strongly believe our actions as humans influence our outcome more than external factors we give credit to.

Your grandmother once told me a story of a Chinese vendor that found her praying in the middle of her daily hustle and bustle on the streets of Guangzhou and said to her *"You Africans.. pray... pray all the time but Africa is still poor.."*

Poor indeed we still are even if we have been the cradle of spirituality and civilization from the beginning of time. It makes you wonder when we took it so far that it created an intellectually dormant and spiritually dependent society.

The cradle of civilization

A historical acknowledgment of our continent as the cradle of civilization cannot be fully recognized without highlighting the history of spirituality on the continent. It radiated in our beautiful languages, our traditional rituals, our entire way of life. There is not a single African language or tribe that did not recognize the presence of a higher power long before Christianity and Islam made its way to the continent. African people had long built societies governed by altruism and the belief in a supreme deity irrespective of cultural domain. Oludumare, Akan, Osirus, Baya, Basuto, Adjuru, Isis, Obatala, Ambo were all complex tribal manifestations of a supreme being akin to the concept of God as we know it today. Our spiritual systems were more layered than both Arabs and Europeans could comprehend leading to a deep level of misunderstanding about its vibrancy on the continent. "Black Magic" as they called it. The enigmatic approach to spirituality that was always more mythical and magical than it was philosophical; was more oral and performative than it was based on scripture. Charms, offerings, and respect for ancestral spirits deeply entrenched in the practices and served as a guiding principle of moral character.

I remember growing up in The Gambia and always feeling the presence of an ancillary layer of spirituality in our traditional myths, superstitions, and magical manifestation. A constant quest for good fortune and battle against the "evil of society" that permeated beyond the traditional Islamic practices. The pillars of Islam that governed the majority of society were not the alpha and omega of our belief systems. Our traditional belief systems which were normally passed on from generation to generation via oral folklore was deeply intertwined with societal norms even if never translated into any text or philosophy. I always found it peculiar that the most pious amongst us had an "all-star" (or two, or three) Marabout man (Serign/"borom Hamhamm") whose reputation and legend created an extra layer of protection that was of utmost importance. The juju beads, holy waters (Safarah) and charms they made were sought after and treated like essential armor. Within communities, misfortunes of people that may have been due to natural causes, lack of personal accountability, medical conditions or ailments not clinically treated were easily attributed to evil works of a *"domah"/"Buaaa"*(witch/wizard). Social outcasts and people with manifestations of mental disorders such as bipolar disorder and schizophrenia were deemed as being possessed by the evil spirits or believed to have suffered consequences of a spell or evil offering casted on them. No social class was immune to such a mental construct. We may not have called our traditional belief systems "religions" from a monotheistic point of view, but one must admit the multi-layered dimension to our spirituality.

The ambiguous overlap between appropriate Islamic rituals and local folklore, which was not only prevalent in The Gambia but also in neighboring countries such as Senegal and Mali, has always existed.. African interactions with Arab merchants exposed them to the way of life (Islam) and worship that was palatable especially in parts that needed a monotheistic unifying form of worship. A spiritual packaging that was readily acceptable by West African Kings and from a diplomatic standpoint helped strengthen ties that were economically beneficial to both parties. The region gradually embraced Islam as a unifying force even if the convergence did not get rid of traditional practices of spirituality (religion) that became laced with Islam. The region craved for spiritual proximity and cultural familiarity to the divine leading to massive subcultures and sects such as the Mourides and Tijans (Sufi Muslim Brotherhoods) rising out of the Senegambia region. To this day, many Mourides, in particular, have become religious fanatics of their spiritual leader Cheikh Amadou Bamba (Serign Touba) viewed as a prophet-like figure. Emboldened with a sense of righteousness, the city of Touba, Senegal to them is the only holy city worth making a pilgrimage to. Such a religious phenomenon is one of many illustrations of how monotheistic religions themselves have gradually evolved and morphed into cultural and regional manifestations similar to ancient Africa.

Some days I wonder if Africa labeled a "Dark Continent" regarding our belief systems should be rejected at all cost? Perhaps our enchantment stems not from a lack of enlightenment but a matrix of mystery encapsulated from within. We accepted new innovations of religions that we have struggled for centuries to find a representation of divinity and spirituality that was like us. When people speak of the "Holy Lands" or birthplaces of religions as history narrates them: Christianity has Europe, Islam the Arabian Peninsula, Buddhism and Hinduism in Asia. All religions mentioned above created and sustained a nonnegotiable narrative and visual representations of divinity that mirrored and radiated cultural elements similar to their own people.

However, on the African continent, religion was merely left mythical at best. Spirituality through monotheistic religion was colonized on the continent of Africa leaving behind a notion of "darkness" that may simply be a large shadow looming over our continent. A tenebrous projection of our constant prostration to absorb "light" (spiritual enlightenment) that is foreign and a lack of propagation and illumination of our true spirit that radiates from within. Sometimes I wonder how our beloved continent would not remain poor, confused, dysfunctional and self-deprecating when we constantly bargain away any source of enlightenment Africans know and understand to be essential to our resilience. We have come to embrace Islam and Christianity in good faith because there's truth in the teachings and being spiritually inclined is part of our true essence as a people. Our societies were built on altruism, and our approach to God, religion, and spirituality could never be confined into one monolithic group.

Your father's journey

I do not have a vivid recollection of an exact awakening ("light bulb") moment I understood the concept of God as a child but have always felt his presence as the guiding light in my world. Religions, God, spirituality, were all concepts ushered into by my environment from birth. The quest of doing more good deeds than bad was part of a philosophical and societal upbringing often unquestioned and unchallenged.

Some of my first recollections of a distinction in faith came during my primary school days at St Joseph's Ex-pupils Primary School. A school influenced by postcolonial Christian missionaries that had always maintained a stellar academic record and produced the nation's brightest students.

Our School assembly always began with The Lord's prayer and the Quranic verse Al- Fatihah. The dichotomy of our school prayers in hindsight had a profound psychological effect on us that imprinted an "us and them" cognitive association when it came to the concept of God. We spoke the same local languages, ate the same local foods, believed in the same tribal traditions, folklore and superstitions yet had a pursuit of piety and an understanding of God that was distinctly different. The crowd of Muslim students fell silent as the words " Our Father, who art in heaven...." filled the air as did the Christian students when "Bismillahi Rahmani Raheem......." was being recited. the lesson period came about, the Christians in the class went one way to learn about the Bible while the Muslims had the school's Oustass (Quranic teacher) walk in for our session. Our Society had established the English language in schools, government and all official matters yet the word of God and the Quran was being taught from Arabic text irrespective of our level of literacy. Confusing, I know, but Islamic studies came with a heavy reliance on translations and transliterations. The manifestation of the Muslim way was more influential from a societal standpoint than it was an individual understanding of what the Quranic verses we recited actually meant. Imagine speaking English in class, learning about God in Arabic and going home to speak Wolof and Mandinka predominantly. Quite the linguistic gumbo soup of ideas and concepts that often got lost in translation.

Most parents similar to mine had a private Oustass come to the house over the weekend to teach the Quran to us. I use the word "teach" lightly because it was more a constant practice in memorization than it was an actual analysis of what the book offered. As I look back at it now as an adult, it's still the most fascinating phenomenon of faith in the unknown that still happens today. The idea of "learning" the Quranic verses in complete blindness. Most of us can recite verses on verses of the Quran from memory without a clue about what the verses actually translate to. We use verses to perform our daily prayers with blotchy comprehension of what every single Arabic word we utter actually means. However,in the midst of such blindness lies a level of deep connection to God which was and is enough spiritual food for our souls. Recitation of the memorized Quranic verses slowly becomes subconscious as we dive deep into a peaceful state of meditation. A feeling of vulnerability to God's awareness of all your thoughts, fears and deepest desires of your heart.

Our religious ecosystems were built around the fear of God, and it shaped all our pursuits of righteousness. Quranic teachers and religious Imams were tasked at giving unquestioned interpretations of the Quran and the life of the prophet Muhammed (Peace be upon him) that molded our young minds and hearts to seek more good deeds than bad. Society, on the other hand, dictated a confusing and sometimes hypocritical calibration of which Muslim "sin" was greater and more denounced than others. Most families had Marabout men that created charms and holy bath waters that "cured and healed" all things in the name of God. The practice of modern scientific medicine often took a back seat to pursuits of spiritual healing. Young Muslims who partook in sins of the youth such as premarital sex and gambling were held to a more forgiving standard than the blasphemy and shame of a young Muslim caught with a bottle of beer. Older men who physically abused and cheated on their wives with sometimes women the age of their daughters often received a blind eye or selectively used the Quran and the Islamic polygyny practices to justify their transgressions.

Yet in the midst of all these imperfect and conditionally convenient pursuits of the religion was an unwavering faith in God as the controller of all things. Islam (95%) and Christianity (5%) helped create a country filled with God-fearing people and a partiality for goodwill that was synergistic with our cultural values. Like many other African societies, Gambian society has always been a praying society. We seek prayer from our parents, and elders, and leave little room for any state of spiritual contentment among people.

I am blessed to have had Islam as a foundation to build discipline and a healthy relationship with God. I am equally blessed to have African morals and values mutually exclusive to Islamic teachings, instilled in me to serve as my moral compass. My innocence and herd-like conformity to Islamic norms growing up gave way to a life of modesty that protected me from many dangerous pursuits of worldly desires and weaknesses of mankind. As I've grown older, however, I have come to realize a level of logic and rationale must be assigned to an interpretation of religion and texts that were constructed centuries ago when mankind was faced with different quandaries of human morality and conduct. I have reached a point of intellectual maturity that makes questioning and choosing not to conform to certain aspects of the religion void of a guilty conscience due to a level of spiritual clarity. Islam and religion as a whole to me was designed and delivered to mold and influence human behavior in a way more good than evil permeates the world. Some individuals who claim the religions may have failed humanity, but the purity of the word of God, irrespective of religion can never be tainted. A strong individual relationship with God will shield your heart and mind from the many ways religions itself can be used against you or your fellow human.

The light in you

My desire to make an honest attempt at explaining all these complexities is in hopes that when you do experience them, you can both appreciate its richness but also be non-negotiable with your belief in the God that is already in you. Even if you succumb to bathe in special holy water and seek blessing from gifted religious scholars, do so with a level of pragmatism that prevents you from hitching your hopes and dreams on the enchantment of a fellow human being.

Science, in particular, has allowed us to discover, study, understand and predict so many aspects of our lives that centuries ago held a special place in the realms of spiritual manifestations. Unexplainable perhaps, but may simply be further manifestations of God's magnificence channeled through the beings of mankind with the creativity and innovations they breathe life into.

There will always be elements in our life we simply cannot explain. What we feel can have a tendency to strike the chords of our internal spiritual instrument and that should be okay too.

As you grow up in this world my child, I pray for you to make it a point of duty to always spread love and kindness while seeking and living only the truth. Your truth. You will be raised as an African who is Muslim true to the definition of the word. (One who surrenders to the will of God.) Read and understand the religious text to find your individual meaning and medium to build a spiritual connection to God. Questioning and using logic to interpret religion will not make you defiant but will only bring you closer to finding true meaning in the word of God. A meaning that stems not from doctrinal conformity but from introspective spiritual exploration.

Understand time and space with respect to your African heritage and spiritual inclination knowing no one race has exclusive rights to God's grace and favor. Growing up in America and the western world in general, the color of your skin that radiates your ancestry will mostly dictate peoples' initial impression and treatment of you more than your religious affiliation. I urge you to remain rooted and non-transactional in your identity as a black African Queen and use Islam and the beauty of its manifestation as building blocks to a foundation of compassion and benevolence towards all of humanity. Build a reputation as a doer of good that transcends all affiliations.

Trust that no human being can ever cast judgment on who God favors and who he doesn't. Spirituality should be seen as a fax machine with God on the receiving end. All religions use a different color pen on a white sheet of paper and hit send. When it comes through the fax machine God only sees black ink on white paper. The content of the message on the paper- individual deeds and spiritual relationship-is all God cares about, not the color of the ink (your religion or language) used.

God created a curious soul in you and I hope you never lose that curiosity to seek knowledge. I will be here to guide you along the way as I was guided by your grandparents using religion (Islam) as an instrument to mold a disciplined life of kindness ,compassion and decent values. I will also be intentional about blank pages left open for you to write your own thesis of how you see and manifest your spirituality.

But for now, enjoy the lightness and innocence you experience especially in times like these that the world seems to be turning upside down. God is still limiting the threshold of your worries to the basic elements of food, comfort, attention and an ever-blossoming personality. Your innocence and pure ability to express emotion without any inhibitions is itself a spiritual manifestation you may not fully appreciate until you are older.

Live true to your name A'isha *(She who lives..)* and always remember that the God we go lengths to find…. is and will always be in you.

Love you more than life itself. You screaming "Dahdeeeeeee! when you see my face pop up is literally oxygen to me.

Daddy

Isha learning to take her first steps around a house full of inventory for daddy's entrepreneurial journey

CHAPTER FOUR

CURSE OF AMBITION

(Written August 2020)

I used to think I inherited broad shoulders and a tall statue from your great grandfather Mankamang Badjie, who hailed from Kankurang (Bwaim) and settled in Bansang where your Grandfather was born five days into the new year in 1950. For 34 years of my life, I heard nothing but legendary stories of his conquests. The stoic warrior and man of the people who pollinated a new settlement (Bansang) with a diversity of tribes interwoven into a beautiful tapestry that cloaked a vast area from the shores of the river banks stretching way past the hills of the rich lands.

All the stories told to me as a child growing infused a warrior-like spirit trying to channel his greatness despite the truth serum of tragedy laced in his story and that of your grandfather's lineage that I am finally getting a dose of.

Being away from you and having intimate moments with your grandfather (my dad) has given me a peek into layers of his life I never knew. A 9-month reintroduction to a man I spent my entire life seeing through the lens of a distinct feature of his design I inherited, his ambition.

A level of ambition that I can trace back to his father and how he built an individual legacy so great, a tragic implosion was inevitable as his over a dozen children of mostly women and five boys *(your grandfather being the youngest of the boys)* struggled to maintain the essence of his human experience beyond his worldly possessions.

Your Grandpa's ambition came from a place of desperation with his beloved father transitioning to the afterlife when he was barely ten years old. This left him with a recalcitrant chip on his shoulder required to bulldoze through a toilsome African patriarchal and polygamous matrix. One that often saw men of great wealth and many children pass away with no succession plan and equal distribution of agency through inheritance. The daughters in the family wallowed away into destitute while the older male children wrestled over the spoils of their fallen father.

Ambition was the key coding my father used to build a level of sinew that allowed him to be that rose that grew from concrete. All the prickly thorns on his stalk cushioned by a subconscious avoidant style of attachment that only highlighted the vibrance of his blood red petals as we *(his children)* gazed on from an emotional distance. Our imperfectly perfect pillar of strength and kindness.

He found in your grandmother a life partner who kept watering that rose bud through the concrete with a magic potion of love and patience. An angelic level of dedication and care that in turn created children wired with an abundance of love but filled with the same level of ambition that was a mere survival mechanism defect in him.

A profound transmission of a trait I found strangely familiar, realizing now how much of him is in me. It scares me as much as it provides a deeper frame of reference of my constitution.

Peeling back the layers of my relationship with your grandfather has made me realize I always saw him through the lens of his aspirations, career and status in society. When the world saw him as *"Commissioner/Governor"* so did I. When he was *"Ambassador Badjie"*, he was to me. Hell, I still call him "H.E." (His Excellency) because the things I had the most depth of knowledge about him growing up were his career accomplishments and an ever burning ambition. He was my *Mr. Miagi* that defied all the odds against him to give us a life full of opportunities. The chief engineer behind my limitless mindset who injected that same curse of ambition into my veins. He knew it was a prerequisite to navigate a sometimes lonely and unforgiving world, even if it came at a price.

In the true nature of our relationship, I find it unusually fitting that he now also refers to me only as *"Dr. Badjie"*. Ambition, achievement and defying the odds has always been our love language. A comfort-ridden flotation device used to avoid diving to the depths of life's heaviness on the both of us knowing the inherent flaws in our emotional design. Our love language, like many African homes, was never one that created a safe space for us to articulate caliginous moments in our lives. Depression, anxiety or a crumbling emotional fortress masked as mere fatigue from home, school or work because of a quiescent relationship built on seeking and giving approval.

What many of my generation may consider coldness in our fathers' emotional warehouses can merely be decades of unattended pent up trauma navigating a society that promoted toxic masculinity and most aspects of emotional intelligence deferred to our mothers.

An inherent flaw in our design I wish to CLTR+ALT+DEL as I start my journey with you. These complexities are why I warned you against men of grand ambition in my previous letter to you.

Ambition always comes at a steep price and will always play interference with your human experience. Looking back at so many of my past relationships, the one trait that was always nonnegotiable was my unrelenting focus on personal goals. A driving force that made every journey a spiritual warfare of willing things into existence, by any means necessary even if it left casualties with faces of neglected loved ones.

Your vibrant presence in my life, however, has made me realize the *"burning a candle on both ends"* effect too much ambition causes. An excruciating zero-sum game that makes standing ovations for milestones feel like a celebration of my misery and deep yearning for your tactile interaction.

I am constantly in a state of reflection, knowing a natural disposition that may seem so appealing to those around me means the least to me right now. All triumphs feel like disasters when you feel the shackles of ambition from fathers' past haunt you down like the grim reaper as you fight to break free from the intoxicating cycle.

I need you to realize that behind this tall frame of mine I inherited from your grandmother lies mine fields of insecurity, anxiety and vulnerability with the daily price you are paying from my ambition as I write this letter.

Peace and happiness has become more and more aspirational when the urgency of fulfillment comes with knowing my time on earth is an inverted hourglass.

Each tiny grain of human experience fading into oblivion is a calculated choice between making memories with people that matter or chasing after that ever moving target of self actualization.

Striving to build a lasting legacy in our current society through our work often comes with a foolish assumption that there is *"quality time"* with the people we love on the other side of fulfillment. Death has a sobering way of reminding us of the contrary. I will tell you stories of the great Kobe Bryant and my love for him when you grow older. In him we saw a man dedicate two decades of his life to chasing generational greatness with an unrelenting sense of impatience with his ambition. A feat that came at a steep price to a family that patiently waited for a post-retirement life of contentment and memories, never a part in God's script.

His sudden departure from the world when he was only 41 years old is a cruel and tragic anecdote of ambition that haunts me every single day.

I hope and pray that a balanced and a healthy dose of ambition would have been instilled in you by the time your eyes read and reflect on this letter.

The impatience with my work now, I've realized, is a constant race against the calcification of your memories of me being constantly away. I'll always wish I could get some moments of your infancy back, but reorientation of my compass would not have happened without the pain absence has caused. You are my true north.

I still believe there's something spiritual in losing oneself in the service of others, but only a cup full of contentment can spill over in a continuous stream. My ambitious traits may very well be coded in you already like it was in me, but one can hope a level of nurturing will calibrate and tame its visceral nature to make room for the people you will also grow to love.

I love you more than life itself and my greatest ambition will always be for you to grow to know my authentic self, not as the world may see me but just as your perfectly imperfect father.

Love,
Daadeeeee

Call me Ismaila
(I am Gambian)

CHAPTER FIVE

HIGHLY SCHOOLED AND UNEDUCATED

(Written December 2017)

From D class to A Class

It is astonishing how profound an impact my earliest schooling at St. Joseph's Ex-Pupils Primary School (better known simply as Mrs. Ndow's) had in shaping the student I saw myself as for the entirety of my academic journey. Our move back home to The Gambia coincided with the third term of the second-grade year which relegated me to the only class that had space for a new student — the D-Class. Being more consumed with adjusting to my new life and environment than I was about how good a student my teachers thought I was, I was totally oblivious to the implications of such a relegation. I had a solid foundation in math and reading from kindergarten in New Rochelle, New York, and my parents had always created a nurturing environment for me to flourish academically.

Something happened the following school year which was the first term of primary three. The administration informed my parents about my results from the previous term which they deemed "superior" enough to move me to "A-class" where I remained for the remainder of my primary school days.

A-class was different. It's where I finally readjusted to the nuances of life back home and started making lasting friendships. A-Class comprised students considered the brightest in their class year. Every aspect of the school system reminded us of our academic prowess and we acted and performed accordingly. All through primary school, the same group of 10 to 20 students were lauded as the "jangist" (Wolof jargon for a smart pupil) and the intense competition amongst us created our separate bubble within the entire class environment. National exams at the 6th, 9th, and 12th grades were no different. It was always the same group of students (including me) that had their names announced across the nation and the fastest way to fame was seeing and hearing your name in the news-papers and radio as being "first, second, or third in The Gambia". Our approach to schooling was that of an academic elitist, and the psychological reinforcement from our teachers, principals, and peers programmed us to believe that every curriculum placed in front of us would have to submit to our natural dominance. We had constant interactions with kids from B-class to D-class during extra-curricular activities but their overall experience was quite different. The school environment instilled in them the belief that they were academically inferior, and as a result they were relegated to a lifetime of calibrated educational potential very early in their development. It's truly remarkable how such an ecosystem existed in an institution designed to provide knowledge and opportunity indiscriminately.

Being a "good student" back then was synonymous with one's knack for conforming to school rules and any proclivity for freedom of thought and expression led to public humiliation and punitive consequences of a physical nature. One dared not challenge or question the status quo. You quickly became the notorious menace who received routine floggings in front of the class or the entire school assembly in some cases. Most of our parents and guardians mortgaged away critical aspects of discipline and the molding of our fragile minds to an educational system that aspired to be the nation's true north post-colonialism. The rigid structure of the school system was unforgiving to any students whose low performance was simply a by-product of a lack of formidable foundation at home either financially or intellectually. At such critical junctures in our mental and emotional development, the idea of being "less than" or "not as intelligent" was slowly downloaded into our internal hardware as viruses select and fortunate few enjoyed the constant priming of their self-confidence and their sense of unlimited potential. What was then deemed "competitive" was nothing more than a systematic way of stratifying the young students' calibration of their own intelligence through an open and in-tentional hierarchical system.

The concept of school uniforms itself was quite the facade for creating an aura of inclusivity. The public categorization of children's intellectual potentials was highly visible, yet so much effort was placed on every student's appearance ensuring that they all looked the same from a bird's eye view. It was normal to tell an 8-year-old that he or she was "D-class talent" but that same student dare not deviate from the white socks and brown sandals in any way that compromised uniformity. Thinking independently was not an all-inclusive feature of the design. The model was built on conformity in thought, discipline/obedience and an overarching ability to read, remember, regurgitate, pass and sometimes purge immediately. Some elements of science and mathematics presented challenges of critical thinking, but in essence an ability to memorize (not analyze or fully comprehend) made you a great student.

The version of history we learned in The Gambia was also whitewashed in the sense that we underwent 12 years of schooling with little understanding of the historical plights of our people and how slavery, genocides and colonialism forever changed our economic predisposition in comparison to the western world. Yes, we knew about Kunta Kinteh, for example, as he was in fact Gambian, but we lacked proper context and awareness of the generational systems of oppression faced by our brethren in the diaspora, especially in America. This intentional lack of continuity in teaching our shared history and heritage did tremendous damage to the once intertwined fabric of the African people. The cultural rift and lack of reciprocal appreciation today between Africans on the continent and those in America did not happen accidentally. It was inevitable. Unless one was privileged enough to have had exposure and education on these subject matters outside of school, you had a very narrow perspective about one another mostly built on devaluing stereotypes.

In the Gambian system specifically, nationalistic ideas were almost impossible to cultivate in a school system that depended mostly on teachers from Ghana, Liberia, Nigeria, and Sierra Leone. If the vision of what it meant to be Gambian and take pride in nation building was absent in the classrooms, how could the children not grow up thinking that anything foreign was always better? Our schools soon became a reflection of government and society in a sense that everyone assumed their place in the spectrum of opportunity. The urban and more financially stable families simply had access to the best educational resources. Mostly through private schools.

One could make the argument that Gambians and, by extension, Africans place an insurmountable amount of trust in a system of schooling that is antithetical to our cultural ways and was never designed to propagate our rich prehistoric knowledge and capacity from the inside out. Our stronghold during the peak of our civilization was built on a direct transfer of skills and knowledge from adult to children through apprenticeship. Families, communities, and geographic regions specialized in a unique set of skills to provide enough goods and services to become fiscally self-sustaining and valuable traders. When it came to establishing discipline and order, the entire community made sure every child exuded behavior that was becoming of the society. Imperialism and colonialism's greatest psychological success was convincing our ancestors that mass schooling and assimilation into western ideologies was the only way to guarantee a fruitful life for the young generation. A strategy that slowly hijacked the fertile minds of children and set a parental control feature to limit boundaries of thoughts and human capacity. A system that consequently gave an opportunity to a select few at the top funneling generations of young minds into a self-deprecating basin of disenfranchisement and poverty.

Education from Yeya and Papa

At home, there was a strict expectation of academic excellence in school. Growing up, my father could have cared less how athletic I was; he was only concerned about my grades. As I transitioned to adolescence, I became more aware of the subliminal approaches to education being instilled at home. Being a middle child of five afforded me a sense of solitude and sporadic isolation of thought that I desperately lacked and craved in school. Conformity to school norms soon caused tremendous boredom, and I walked around with a million "whys" in my head. I remained in the top tier of students academically but not always because of effort. I could read and commit subject matter to memory and apply them efficiently enough to ace exams thereby keeping my dad off my back. He often could sense my lack of consistent effort -- and so did all my siblings who hated my ability to procrastinate studying exam material until the last minute and yet still pass with flying colors. Looking back at my experience, in my quest for knowledge and meaning I simply saw and considered other aspects of life more intriguing than the monotony of school. I went through so many phases of intense curiosity with pets, drama,theater, trivia, sports and later in high school youth advocacy all of which afforded me invaluable experiences.

After moving back home, my mother had taken over my grandmother's retail shop and rebranded it entirely. It was now "New York Fashion" at №8 Albert Market, in Banjul, where the Fulani traders sat on the steps selling kola nuts and engaging in endless banter with market women and men. Some of my days after school were spent at the retail shop waiting for a ride home. I was always fascinated by my mother's daily encounters and interactions with customers with whom she built relationships around a common desire to look and feel good. In her, I saw a woman who did not need a college degree to demonstrate a superior level of business acumen. She had experience working at a commercial bank but had received great tutelage from my grandmother in all affairs of entrepreneurship. She mastered the dynamics of emotional intelligence in business and so often displayed admirable levels of compassion especially during the holidays. She understood the plight of her fellow women and saw them all worthy of having the very best even if it meant sometimes transacting on credit until they had funds to pay for desired goods.

Summer vacations with her in Harlem, New York were also quite an experience. I remember walking the streets of Broadway in the hot summer sun carrying bags from one Chinese vendor to another watching her negotiate wholesale prices with such precision that she was able to make enough profit to offset all the shipping costs. I could not have received a more hands-on educational experience. My mother's ability to adapt and conduct business with fierce negotiation skills irrespective of the continent she was on or the language she did not speak a word of was truly impressive. These were life lessons that taught me more about business, versatility and a knack for thriving outside one's comfort zone than any school system could have. She approached life with such a disregard for the confines of the society that resonated in us all. She educated us to see value in our individual talents and not in opportunities dangled in front of us by our schools and eventual employees.

Education from my dad came in continuous waves distinctively different from my mother. From my dad, I learned the ability to articulate my thoughts and see any idea presented in front of me worthy of scrutiny. It was a study of bimodal frequencies of a very complex man. On one side was the guy who forced us to watch endless videos of Minister Louis Farrakhan on Sundays not because he necessarily agreed with the entirety of the minister's message, but as a study of a man who had an oratorical adeptness worth emulating. A man whose bravado was laced with an unapologetic articulation of his thoughts and feelings about the powers-that-be. A man who knew his mind was immune to any external influence that came with ulterior motives. My father gave us continuous education on demanding respect through speech and presentation. I also consider myself lucky to have had my dad as my first psychologist way before my schooling started. Reflecting on it as an adult him calling me superman may sound corny, but it had an immense impact in priming me for the world I was about to face. How could a teacher or school system convince me of any limitation when my father relentlessly told and showed me otherwise. He knew me better and always bet on me succeeding.

In his professional life, my father's humility and ability to *"walk with crowds, and keep his virtue, talk with kings, nor lose his common touch"* (to quote Rudyard Kipling's poem *"IF"*) were lessons he constantly instilled in us. He was a man I observed routinely stop, chat and share a cigarette or cup of attaya (Chinese green tea) with guards at the bottom of government buildings on his way up to conduct business with Secretaries of State. He always found a way to connect and acknowledge the presence of his fellow humans irrespective of social status. Some of my fondest memories were the times spent with him in rural areas when he served as Governor in Kerewan, Mansakonko, and Brikama (all Administrative capitals in the North Bank, Lower River, and Western Regions of The Gambia respectively). He had a natural ability to not only speak an array of local languages but always maintain an aura of humility that reinforced humanistic values in us and provided a front row lesson on diplomacy and politics in general. Lessons that were tangible, lessons school could not offer. His teachings on human relations continued well into our adulthood as he transitioned as a career diplomat across the globe.

I remember questioning his decision in 9th grade to break my circle of private school friends, sending me to public school at Gambia High School. It was never about the grades because very little had changed in my academic performance through the 6th and 9th grade national exams. He never had to explain his decision. I lived through his adjudicature as an educational experience. He had created comforts in schooling my entire life that had in turn insulated me from the lives of students from all socio-economic backgrounds. He knew Gambia high School would produce a different experience, add layers of humanity and humility to my growth and forever shape the man I would become. Those three years turned out to be some of the most dynamic times of my career as a student.

Nelson Mandela once said: "Education is the most powerful weapon which you can use to change the world"-

The quest for knowledge driven by a healthy level of curiosity and reasoning has always been the cornerstone of all humanity's evolution.

All innovation indeed came out of necessity fuelled by curiosities about endless possibilities. The concept of school, however, has slowly been diluted and presented as the only source of education when all outcomes of our modern times show evidence to the contrary. We hear countless success stories of social giants of our time who did not secure a college degree. Their narrative of a lack of extended schooling tends to overshadow the immense level of education they received through an obsessive curiosity about a subject matter that led to a vision, thousands of hours of exposure, study, trials, and failures. Influencers of human behavior in the realms of politics, militarism, capitalism, religion, imperialism, and colonialism have throughout history utilized mass schooling as a potter's wheel to mold young minds into obedient servants of society. Children's minds are spun into a frenzy of a constant need for validation and approval; self-esteem twiddled by the framework of a school reward system that slowly shaves off their attention spans to limited dispositions of meeting deadlines and making "honor" rolls.

The desperation of our times demands that society questions, scrutinizes and reforms any schooling system that fails to provide one with a sense of purpose tangible enough to live off while providing society with the benefits of their expertise. The minds of children are to be set free to think independently, to question and explore curiosities without risk of societal humiliation or calibration of potential.

Our parents, our schools, all hammer in our heads *"stay in school, get good grades and graduate so you can get a high paying job to live a good life."* Agreeably the knowledge acquired through such a predisposition can be precious but it also alienates so much of our human experience. Education in its purest form is always an inevitable byproduct of human interaction and exposure. An ever-growing ability to observe, analyze, adopt (or purge), master and reciprocate. That that is an innate tendency of all human beings that from a tender age, build the capacity to exist, evolve and thrive within the means provided to us by our environment.

Psychological priming can be one of the most destructive or explosive boosts to a child's mind. Our future generation deserves a new approach to education, and we must demand more from our school systems. Too many young people are highly schooled but still uneducated searching desperately in an avaricious world, to find meaning and purpose well after years of schooling.

As parents, communities, and nations, we have to be our own curators of the quality and diverse source of education our children receive. It's our only hope of sowing seeds for an enlightened generation to come. Mass schooling should be treated as one of many avenues to a life of meaning and not as the only route. It should be an ecosystem for exploration and acquisition of knowledge to help propel the human race forward and not as a gateway to financial security.

Perhaps institutes of schooling are frankly not failing our children, they are doing precisely what they were intended to do with our endorsement. Help control the population while selling an idea of intellectualism and nobility to the highest bidder in the hope that one of many disciplines provided will help sustain the socio-economic growth of individuals and nations. Schooling, especially at the University level, is now more of a risky business investment than it is a gateway to financial freedom. The only difference is that banks are more willing to give an 18-year-old $50,000 for a degree that will earn him/her a $20,000 a year salary but will not even entertain the idea of a start-up business loan for half that amount.

I dedicated 27 years of my life to schooling just to come to the realization that every attribute that set me apart once I entered the professional realm was something encoded in me thanks to the education I got through my parents and my life experiences. Primary and secondary schools in The Gambia were meaningful in creating a healthy appetite for academic competition, but I benefited immensely from being afforded "A-Class" privileges psychologically. Undergraduate study at Tennessee State University was an academic gateway to a top ten Doctor of Pharmacy program at Purdue and provided invaluable experiences in how to navigate the America I was reintroduced to again as a young black man. The stakes got higher the further I went, and the complexities of my adult life made me evolve as a student. Being at Purdue University was the first time in my life, when school was not the only thing I had to worry about daily. How was I going to find funds for the following semester? What was I to do with the massive debt I was accumulating? How could I afford not working two jobs to survive while taking a full load of classes? How could I leverage my career to improve my family's situation and find my way back home? The frequent naps I was notorious for sneaking in while sitting in the second row of the class were often the only thirty minutes of tranquillity my mind experienced. The weight of all these concerns could have easily rattled the sinews of my core but I was resting on a solid matrix of intellectual confidence and faith built over all these years. My ability to bunker down and focus in the library for 12 to 16 hours the night before an exam and still find a way to make it through had never changed. I had come too far, just to come too far.

I am grateful to have always seen every aspect of my life through a global lens due to my early exposure living on three continents before the age of 15 that created my version of limitless boundaries. All the educational experiences through watching my mother's entrepreneurial spirit and her emotional intelligence with customers inherently made me a better community health care professional today. The vast knowledge in science and medicine along the way were merely ingredients and necessary tools picked up along the way. My father's charisma and ability to relate to people from all walks of life instilled in me a sense of benevolence and humility in me that I am forever grateful for.

I see no shame in seeking knowledge through schooling as a way to contribute to the advancement of the human race. I am clearly a product of it. Being highly educated however, should allocate the mental capacity and enlightenment to question the intentions of the source of one's education ("the who"), assess the manner in which one received their education ("the how"), analyze the content and range of said education ("the what") and most importantly, help determine the purpose of one's education ("your why").

In the words of Albert Einstein "Education is what remains long after one has forgotten what one has learned in school."

Educate, Educate …..Educate.

CHAPTER SIX

REIMAGINING NATIONALITY

(Written February 2021)

Our beloved Gambia turned 56 years old few days ago *(Feb. 18th)* and I couldn't help but marvel at the beautiful tapestry of hues displayed as renditions of *"The Flag... The Face"* that. flooded social media. Gambians of all ages popping up from all corners of the world like a vibrant roll call of solidarity, even if the slideshows were laced with micro doses of vanity.

I pondered for a second whether succumbing to the trend of the day was apt, but could not ignore how dispassionate I felt void of any feelings of joy or celebration when the recurring image of on the left (our flag) kept popping up.

How was I to raise a glass free of mendacity to toast to an independence I've struggled to reconcile with objectively?

What was wrong with me? Was I falling victim to the insidious cynicism most returnees felt after months of grappling with the society's deathless level of recalcitrance towards modern and progressive ideas.

Was my original sin not being indoctrinated as "Gambian" years after only being "African" to the many kids I grew up with in New York prior to returning home?

Did it stem from a lack of patriotism and nontoxic nationalism being instilled in us at schools in the Gambia?

It always felt like the cocktail of tribes in my DNA masked by the veil of my Jola last name, the local language I spoke (or didn't speak) and the religious classroom I entered always meant more than instilling a sense of oneness nationalism should have provided.

The Wolof proverb *"Linga don so kor banyeh, dafa feka nga gen say nyaww"* (vaguely translates to being the worst of your kind if you dislike your kind) kept ringing in my ear on independence day.

Was I the worst version of Gambian to not feel celebratory on that momentous but dusty day? *(Not a joke, Gambia had one of the worst pollution days with the desert dust flooding the streets)*

Each refresh on my timeline sent my conscience for a spin, leaving trails of whispers to the tune of *"Where's your Flag Face, SUMAILA!? Do you not love your country?!"*

Whispers that led to a deep moment of reflection as I sought a level of clarity as to what being "Gambian" even meant.

This experiment of a nation that has been "The Gambia" is only a 56 year old construct. A nation 14 years younger than my father led me to ask what he thought he was when he was 12? Was the idea of nationality still foreign to him?

So let's take an abbreviated journey down memory lane in "HIS" *(not my father's)* version of Gambian history.

"HE" said the first written record of the region came from Arab traders in the 9th and 10th centuries.

"HE" also mentions eras of African greatness in the 13th Century Mali Empire, when great kings Sundiata Keita and Mansa Musa ruled the lands. Stories of magnificent feats filled with melancholic episodes of squandered opportunities to fight against the divide-and-conquer mantra of imperialists.

The region that included Gambia also saw the rise of the Songhai Empire (16th Century) with the likes of Sonni Ali making their mark in the region on the heels of the Mali empire.

Besides the rise and fall of our empires, 15th and 16th century history took an intentional pivot in focus to the Portuguese being listed as the first Europeans to visit the Gambia river. "HE" said English merchants in that era heard of this *"river of secret trade and riches concealed by the Portuguese"*. It begs one to wonder the nature of these *"precious commodities"* worthy of such discretion.

"HE" also highlights the 17th and 18th century, filled with the English and the French playing chess games over our Senegambia colony until the 19th century when Sir Alexander Grant of the British Army "saved" Gambia from becoming a French colony. Re-establishing English power in The Gambia region with the city of Bathurst (Now Banjul).

Our region of the Gambia was then a part of British West Africa with the management structure based predominantly in Freetown, Sierra leone. Our colonial masters leveraged the most educated Africans in the region at the time (the *"Akus"* or *"krios"*) composed of freed slaves and from the west with roots tracing back to the Yoruba people of Nigeria.

A version of British West Africa's *"Talented Tenth"* that created the fabric of a new elite class of Africans with western education capable of consolidating forces with our selected few educated native Gambians of influence. This group formed what became the nucleus of our founding fathers under the leadership of Sir Dawda Kairaba Jawara.

Abbreviated version of how our independence came about, yes, but more pressing questions beg for extended pontification.

Who is "HE" in the narration of Gambian history? A common singularity I noticed as I chased down the different rabbit holes of our history was a glaring confirmation that similar to the entire continent, so much of our history had been narrated from the perspective of a male Arab or White man. Both stories are documented through the nauseating lens of POWER and POSSESION.

The African man was always the accomplice in the story. Getting intoxicated on the two pervasive Ps and to this day; seeking power by any means necessary while maintaining the audacity to believe possession of the nations' wealth, the youths' future and dictating what a woman can or cannot do with her body and agency is a God given right.

Imperialists understood this psychological vulnerability rooted in greed and self preservation. All you needed was ONE African Man of influence to give you keys to the kingdom in exchange for a tiny slice of riches accompanied with an elevation in society as "The chosen one". Remnants of this defect still plague most African countries with deal making done clandestinely and often based on what's in it for the decision making man in power and not the collective nation.

Lost in the entire narration are stories of our human development. Our shared experiences. Our communities led and sustained by women. Our imbued fusion with spirituality free of imperialist ideologies of God. Our sense of identity that did not bend at the knee to the barrel of the maxim gun or a slave whip.

Was our version of governance, community policing and general nimbleness of migration based on greener pastures so broken that a completely foreign concept (Nationality) had to be handed to us not before, but after parts of the continent were offered a la carte to our colonial masters?

Was sovereignty and nationality mutually exclusive back then? So many thoughts come to mind as I reflect on what the intent of granting African nations' independence was? Was the idea of nationality as silly as dividing Senegambia into two nations to implant a differentiating chip in our DNA? How many Gambians can count four generations back and not trace their roots to another part of Africa?

56 years later, the "independent" Gambia's human development index ranks 172nd out of 188; 41% of our population live in multidimensional poverty, only 35% of our population are considered "skilled labor force" and the average Gambian is only living to be 62 years old.

Our country offers Gambian nationals little to no advantages over non gambians in the adaptation of ideas and provision of opportunities. We consume and validate so many elements that are antithetical to this idea of oneness nationality should cultivate. Insidious elements of patriarchy, sexism, tribalism and ageism are as imperious now as they have ever been. As a result, many talented Gambians have given up on the nation and turned to countries and institutions building legacies on the back of their ingenuity while the *"crabs in a bucket"* mentality *(if i can't have it, neither can you)* still stifles our country.

Which begs the questions: (i) what has this borrowed concept of nationality served for us? Whose interest has the 52+ nationalities in Africa served besides sowing division and xenophobia, protecting the influence of our colonial masters and only 1 to 3 percent of natives still operating from a position of power and possession.

I've always considered our dinner table a microcosm of the dysfunction in this borrowed idea of nationality. At the head of the table sits my father *(In his 70s)* who has honorably served all three republics of The Gambia over a 30 year career as a diplomat and civil servant. Yet, in retirement, he still believes his ilk harbor the best ideas of what the nation needs. The nation's political leadership still teeters between men of his age or slightly younger still banking on antiquated 1965 ideas to build ineffectual 2050 versions of our nation while the talented young and women especially, languish away on the sidelines.

Sitting across from him are children and grandchildren that hold 4 different nationalities. A deep love for our people still radiates but the choice of nationality is mostly influenced by nations that provide the best opportunities to strive and benefit from meritocratic systems that push and elevate the best of their own citizens.

So, what does it actually mean to be "Gambian" and what independence is there to celebrate? What are we free from?

We are social constructs. Nationality, like most things in life, such as our religions, names, culture, and gender roles are decided for us minutes after we are born into this earth. Yet, we often spend an entire life defending, conforming and avoiding an uncomfortable grappling with these constructs from a place of logic and reasoning aligned with current realities of the 21st century.

Africa was great when the diversity in our hues, origins and native tongues created an ecosystem where the best of what we did in our respective silos was an economic catalyst that organically manufactured vibrant intellectual melting pots and economic hubs like a Timbuktu.

You know an African when you see one. There's a potent permeation of joint spirits that resonate when we see our kind. It's the spiritual Kora strings of Sona Jobarteh and Sura Susso that awaken your heart. The soulful rhythm of Fela Kuti's percussion echoing the raw emotions of the motherland. It's the circumnavigation of hips induced by the sound of Papa Wemba. The tidal wave of contemporary culture carried by the crooning of Davido's "If I tell you say I love you o!"

Our essence as a people has always been connected like arteries and veins carrying blood pumped from one beating heart to all extremities of our vast lands.

We lost that along the way, temporarily, but we can re-imagine nationality and just be African again.

We can be the generation that dares to mark the idea of different nationalities within Africa as a failed experiment. Our collective allegiance should not be tied to where on the continent one is born, but where we simply choose to call home and add value to society. We can return to a time when exploration fuels opportunities on new frontiers, not restricted by the limits of our immigration laws.

The complexity of such a seismic reconstruction and psychological deprogramming may be far-fetched to some but also begs others to ask: what do we have to lose?

We have enough of a sample size to scrutinize how inept some of these tools handed down to us have been in improving the lives of African people. All our nations have mastered the art of fighting oppression and being antagonist to ruling parties, leaving very little fertile grounds for collaborative socioeconomic development.

Can you imagine the power and dominance one governing union of West Africa can have? Over 300 million people who are void of restrictive elements of nationality. Besides being finally able to settle the longstanding Jollof rice! banter, our collective potential can force a new world order with the abundance of our human and natural resources.

Gambia is great because the region has produced some of the most beautiful people. In those faces next to the flag I see strength in the diversity of our cultures, the distance of our migrations and the pride in our land.

My love for our people will always be the unconditional magnet that draws every sinew of my body home.

But the question remains: what am I?

I am an African born in the Senegambia region. That is the common singularity I share with millions of people irrespective of which one of my two passports *(American and Gambian)* I choose to navigate the world with. It's the one constant in me, regardless of which flag I pledge allegiance to.

Africans will have to be captains of our faith and masters of our destiny.

If we want to go fast as "nations" we can go alone, but if we want to go far and be the most dominant force in the world, we must go together.

Peace and Love.

CHAPTER SEVEN

THE GAMBIA: COUNTRY OF INDIFFERENCE

(Written July 2021)

A tattered flag of The Gambia on a river Gambia boat cruise symbolic of the indifference to proper value and upkeep of our beloved nation.

It's Wednesday, July 21st and I am sitting at our facility in The Gambia wondering how the streets could be so empty with no economic activity on what normally should be the peak of workplace productivity.

Well, it's yet another public holiday. The nation celebrated Eid *(Tobaski)* yesterday and was granted a second day encore for reasons I find hard to reconcile with.

Strange yes, but definitely on brand with a nation that barely works four and a half days a week and has a pervasive and obstinate affinity to low productivity.

In short, we are not a serious nation, and we are completely unbothered by our mediocrity. A country that has no qualms sacrificing 63% of the week to enjoy a feast can never be a formidable player in this competitive global economic landscape. We will always be lambs in a lions' den.

Rich nations like the United Arab Emirates, sure; their nation is wealthy enough to ensure their entire citizenry remains bloated with social safety nets that afford them the luxury of not seeing work as essential to survival

The Gambia, on the other hand, we live in this dystopian matrix where unemployment is the highest it's been in over two decades (11.08% in 2020) and even those with jobs do not make a living wage. Very few Gambians take home $200 (D10,000) a month and live in a depressive cycle of surviving paycheck to paycheck or stuck at the mercy of a loved one in the diaspora to fund their lifestyle via remittance of money. Over $600 Million was sent in 2020 alone to circulate briefly in the country before leaving right out.

Being an employer of over 50 Gambians has also afforded me insight into the insidious psychology of the Gambian worker that our society has molded and enabled for decades. Our wages can be improved but our predilection to disregard standards coupled with non-committal relationships with high productivity are the reason most of our systems do not work.

We are a country of indifference. Indifference to high standards, indifference to high performance, indifference to consistent productivity, indifference to accountability, indifference to high moral character, indifference to transformational ideas, indifference to the grim realities of the COVID—19 pandemic, just indifference.

Time and time again we get lost in superficial political banter and try to *"Mansplain"* all the ills in society but cannot take ownership of our inherent disposition as a people to not care.

The great yogi Sadhguru once said, *"You can change the paint color of a house (to yellow, blue, green, grey or brown in our case) but the foundation remains the same.."*

We the people are the nation's foundation. Our cultures, our behaviors, our work ethic and our moral judgment. Therefore, all of our systems and leaders will always reflect every worn out thread of thew in us, good or bad.

No Messiah or individual leader can solve that. Even in an election year, we owe it to ourselves to calibrate our expectations and realize that the fight is still over who holds the paintbrush and chooses the color of paint and not the blue collar engineer willing to root out the sewer rotting our foundation away. Transformational change will not happen just because we have a new party or president in power. It will be the same crease on a different man's trouser.

We are a nation whose pride seldom lies in not being able to be outworked by a non-Gambian. We are a nation that will frustrate our brightest to abscond with bitterness in their heart. We are a nation that stifles opportunities for our women and youth, wasting away their most formidable years.

It's truly disheartening to realize being "Gambian" offers minor advantages in a land where not a single sector in our economic ecosystem is dominated by "Gambians". *(I challenge you, the reader, to reflect on any sector that we can say "Don't even try, the Gambians dominate that space...")*

All great nations have a robust private sector full of companies and businesses that the entire government infrastructure builds a failure-proof, shock absorber to ensure they become multi-generational companies. Think of all the historic U.S companies like Ford, GM, Boeing for example.

Our African governments, on the other hand, almost assume a competitive or reluctant stance against the local private sector while remaining willing to play ball with foreign entities. Obviously, our nation cannot develop without foreign investment and collaboration but it shouldn't leave our budding local companies at a competitive disadvantage all the time.

I have returned home and stuck around long enough to see how since independence, much of our "regulations" and bureaucratic systems have been a revolving appraisal of "WIIFMs" *(What's in it for me)*. Being an entity dedicated to job creation and building human capacity is cute but most decision-makers realize the merry-go-round nature of their positions and are in it to maximize personal gains while the cushy seat remains theirs. They have dedicated their entire careers to the horrendous wages of the civil service in a *Hunger Games* survival of the fittest environment so any slither of opportunity leaves little room for morality. The welfare of their families depend on the spoils.

I believe corruption is a feature of every type of governance, democratic or not. Poverty just exacerbates the tendency to tilt the scale more toward pilferage than nation building. Our appointed heads of government institutions are easy targets to castigate but some of them are shackled by dense multilayered systems of corruption and sabotage even if they have pure intentions of executing the will of the people.

Our government has relinquished its responsibility as the catalyst for economic growth, entrusting it instead to donor organizations whose primary goal of alleviating poverty has yet to demonstrate a credible path towards sustainable prosperity. The aid they provide has been harshly criticized as "dead aid" for precisely this reason. It is disheartening to imagine how many government officials have benefited from funds intended for the nation, with extravagant homes and lavish college tuitions financed through cunning and nefarious methods of inflating project costs, ensuring that all parties involved do not need to ask, " What's in it for the boys?!" or as the Gambian Ndongos would say "ah, nakala nak?"

Many non-Gambian entities with bottomless wallets, therefore, realize African decision-makers have "a price" or at the minimum, a healthy level of curiosity about potential spoils from a deal. They cut to the chase, ensuring their agenda focuses on the right palms being greased and not goodwill proclamations of the number of Gambians that would earn employment and upward mobility because of their establishment.

Any individual seeking fertile ground in The Gambia sees the plethora of problems as opportunities for revenue-generating solutions. Once they get acquainted with the psychology of the people, our lack of competitive discipline, disloyalty to our fellow compatriots and low overall productivity, it's game over. Give them half a decade and they would have amassed generational wealth while investing very little in the human development of our sleeping, smiling coast.

We have a vast number of non-Gambian owned private entities that do not even spend 5% of their total revenue on competitive wages to Gambian people. Reality is most deem our talent/work ethic unworthy of dignified pay and know our regulators are drenched in conflicts of interests to assume any position other than indifference.

One doesn't have to be a trained economist to see the utter lack of social responsibility from economic vultures in the market but even the Gambian people assume a position of indifference and still choose to spend their dalasi in businesses they never see hire, train and/or develop our people. The Gambian dalasi leaves the Gambian community faster than a covid-infested currency note makes it into a mask-less bank teller's bare hands.

Our Gambian businesses have room to improve the quality of service and consistency, but frankly our entire service industry is built on indifference. It's a *"lor buga?" (what do you want?)* culture in most places of business and never *"how may I be of service today?."* Their indifference is balanced on the regressive notion that customers will pay for products and services they have to offer regardless, so why offer an experience indicative of their appreciation.

We have a long way to go and our country can be a hard place to love when every crack of dawn presents an intractable fog of peremptory stagnation.

One only draws solace in a budding resistance forming in front of us. The members of the Gambian Renaissance who refuse to let indifference seep into their awakened crevices. Bright minds, both home-bred and returnees from the diaspora, being intentional about bringing the fight into the arena with armories full of transformational ideas and a recalcitrant resistance to mediocrity. Our "talented tenth" that can will the change they want to see into existence. Set of individuals who have flushed hope and aspirational serendipity down the toilet and are taking a pragmatic approach to solving problems and creating value in spite of all the sludge of Gambian existence.

Holding on to hope. The idea of "holding on to hope" in itself has always been a problematic exercise in futility for us Gambians. It doesn't work. Never has.

Holding on to hope is why our fertile river banks are left untilled while our youth idly fantasize about a fairytale of a life abroad after flaming out of a school system that leaves close to 90% of students ineligible for university.

Holding on to hope is why our society turns a blind eye to the physical, verbal and emotional abuse of women in their marriage homes by men enabled and made immune to accountability by our cultural and religious norms.

Holding on to hope is why the poorest village in the country may not have running water, electricity or a vocational training center but have a couple of shiny mosques or churches.

God doesn't love us more than he does his 7.674 billion humans living in the world. He helps those who help themselves. Our nation has remained underdeveloped because we, the people, have not picked ourselves up by the bootstrap to build it.

Hope without intentional change in mindset, behavior and action is meaningless. Nothing gets better until one does something about it.

Our version of hope is a melancholic cliffhanger that never has an expiration date. The entire country and continent has been hopeful and prayerful for generations while the world is choosing a more fruitful disposition than hope (action) and leaving us behind.

What we need more of is simply action, execution, implementation, and accountability!

Until we (the people) care enough about exhibiting a collective commitment to excellence and high productivity, we will forever be a stagnant nation.

Sunj deka bi du dem! (Our nation will be stagnant forever!)

If we love it, we have to be honest about it.

Being of Gambian descent is something we cannot change, but our Gambian mindset of indifference is something we have to factory reset and install an updated processing system.

CHAPTER EIGHT

EXEMPLARY YOUTH

(Written March 2022)

As the knot on the evening's black silk bow tie unfolded, I couldn't help but reflect on a night full of so many thoughts and emotions.

I had so much I wanted to say on stage but kept it short because God forbid long acceptance speeches getting in the way of the King of Mballax, Youssou Ndour.

To begin, I am humbled and honored to have been nominated, voted for, and awarded with the 2021 Fatu Network's Heroes Award for the Exemplary Youth of the year. To everyone involved in the process, Thank you.

To my fellow Nominees: Marr Nyang and Youssou Sisawo, congratulations. I am inspired by your work. You both are stars in your own right and equally deserving of the award.

With my head constantly kept down with blinders on, chipping away at the daunting task of building a startup company, I must admit that there was a level of discomfort that initially came with my awareness of the award nomination.

The first thing I did was google *"What age range is considered youth?"*. There was a level of humor in my discovery that it was in fact 18 to 35 because Gambia and Africa, in general, is a place where an adult could be married, with a child, 10-year career, and male pattern baldness (in my case) and still be considered "Youth".

The irony is 2021, which was my 35th year on earth, would have been well past the halfway point of my life based on the grim reality of the average Gambian man's life expectancy not being above 63 years old.

We are not living long enough yet society has a ubiquitous way of dissipating our most vibrant years of productivity and potential economic vibrancy (25 to 45) on an imaginary launch pad with limited access to rocket fuel kept as paper coupons by discretionary gatekeepers.

My secondary layer of discomfort was grappling with the anxiety that comes with anything to do with the title of "Hero". An individual admired for his moxie and achievements. Admiration and lionization that can often be rooted in a deep misunderstanding of the complexities of a human being's experience in the Gambia.

I, therefore, always seek more prayers and protection from my parents when any abundance of recognition is thrown my way. It scares me simply because it puts make-up over a weary soul bruised, bloodied but unbowed.

It always takes a village and God's grace to produce what is deemed material success in a person.

The Gambia has a way of seeing what is considered as "Light" lit from the flames of our creator too bright to warrant your fellow human attempting to dim it down a notch. And this is me speaking from a position of privilege as a man in a patriarchal society. Lord knows how difficult the plight of a young talented shining star of a Gambian woman is.

My Innovarx journey in The Gambia since December of 2019 has felt like an ongoing Jihad full of trials. From warning letters of closure and orders to stop advertising our health services from the Ministry of Health *(perfectly fine for a traditional healers posted up at the trade fair marketing to thousands of people about concoctions that heal all things but death)*, a lack of official recognition as a health facility, begging to provide efficient COVID-19 vaccination services free of charge to the public to a more recent intentional refusal for our company *(with the best digital health platform)*, to conduct basic COVID-19 rapid antigen tests for traveling citizens in a convenient and highly efficient manner like the rest of the world.

Young minds with ideas backed by good intentions of creating value and improving the lives of citizens shouldn't require a constant Herculean effort to simply stay alive.

The Gambia, to my knowledge, is the only country that not a single private sector company was allowed to participate in providing any COVID-related service and it makes you wonder why?

Why can the Medical Research Council (MRC) *(Nothing against the reputable institution)* provide a service considered acceptable but Innovarx cannot?

Why can't an individual traveling to a destination that simply requires a rapid antigen test schedule an appointment online at *www.igh.com, while sitting* at home or at their hotel, and have the Innovarx Wellness on Wheels team show up and provide the service in 15 minutes leaving them with a hassle-free digital record/certificate to spend the last hours of their travel preparations with loved ones?

And, yes, we have had the technology and know-how to provide that exact experience for the last 9 months but refused approval.

Our company lost over 1 million Dalasis ($20,000) of potential revenue in February 2022 alone being barred from providing services to tourist travelers with no valid justification. The glee and satisfaction in airport health officials shaming our company name to travelers and airlines alone makes one realize how pedestrian it is for us to tear down what is ours.

You mean to tell me fraudulent practices of selling negative COVID-19 results are more likely to happen in a newly found private company with everything to lose from a reputation standpoint, than as currently constituted?

Do you know how many Gambian youths a private company could have provided meaningful jobs to with dignified pay if such a service was done at scale?

Thus, behind that smile on stage that night was a brewing broken heart and weary body from navigating all the sludge in our system.

It's easy to politicize things and point fingers at elected officials but we are still a nation void of any home-court advantage because our people still don't intuitively root for our own. In a land of limited resources and prostituting of our problems *(to foreign donors)*, the ground will always be barren soil for any viable solutions to germinate from the private sector.

I've simply survived the past years by leaning on the fundamental belief that my purpose of creating value through positive health experiences and prolific human development of my staff is simply me assuming my position as God's instrument for the limited time I have. The unknown amount of sand in my inverted hourglass gives a great sense of urgency and impatience knowing *body no bi firewood*.

The Gambia has always been a mental, spiritual, and emotional training ground for creating value across the continent and showing the world that young African minds are capable of making excellence in service a way of life. My experience is not unique to me, nor am I any more special than the many frustrated entrepreneurs and young professionals facing trials.

I have to communicate an honest depiction to spark a much-needed dialogue in our nation right now. Suffering in silence in our respective industry silos will not incite change.

Candle in the dark. I use the candle in the dark/stars analogy to describe the state of our youth in this nation.

A candle never loses its brightness by lighting another candle yet so much of our psyche cannot look past more than one_____ existing. From our traditions, religions, and political infrastructure we do not value strength in numbers that transcend a cult of personality around one individual.

So we innately maintain a culture of taking a defensive posture by sucking the oxygen out of any room that another candle has an opportunity to be lit, not knowing that a simple ripple effect of candles being lit, stars being found can create a galaxy that can finally compete on a global scale.

Our country is sombre enough (literally!) for ten thousand candles/stars to go ablaze at the same time! Anyone flying over the Gambia in the wilderness of the dark will suddenly take notice of a permeating brightness across all sectors.

A simple science experiment will show you that no matter how bright a candle is, suck the oxygen out of the environment and the flame dies away. The same experiment will also show that a lit candle has a finite amount of time to lean over and light other candles with longer stems next to it before its wax slowly melts away into obscurity.

Take a minute to digest that analogy and there lies the thousands of youth (candles with long stems) waiting to be lit into a Gambian Galaxy.

The Gambia has always had stars *(Lit Candles)*. We have a youthful population yet wonder why so many of our candles feel deprived of the oxygen needed to multiply into a generation of Gambian Galaxies that can take the nation to new frontiers.

My "candle" was lit, and is continuously lit, by the flames of so many stars that positively impacted my life have been extinguished. Countless Gambians older and younger than me that never get a chance to get their roses. This award is a direct reflection of their grace.

I see your light and encourage you to keep turning your flame into a bonfire.

I look around disheartened to see an entire generation of candle flames before me that floated away across seas like a funeral ritual to be reincarnated in other societies as bonafide stars that never return as comets.

This "Exemplary Youth award", ultimately belongs to all 60+ employees of Innovarx Global Health.

We are a youthful organization delivering excellent and inspired work I am so proud of. The company is full of youth in their 20s and early 30s at all levels. Over 70% of our leadership positions are held by a woman and that is a mere reflection of the current calibration of talent in our country. Our company is truly sustained by the grit and minds of some of the most talented young people.

My team inspires me so much that it makes fighting a good fight and doing things in spite of _____, worthwhile. We embrace how flooded with obstacles the road has been but remain committed to filling every unforgiving minute with intentional efforts at creating value for our people. A company full of stars or better yet NOVAS!

We live by one mantra: *"head down and keep peppering with excellence!"*

Lastly, I want to also thank all my family members who have had a front-row seat for every experience good or bad. My daughter and wife who know the toll of a dad always on the road. Their steadfast love and support have been an anchor. A trusting safety net that has caught and propelled me back into the air so many times after being knocked down.

That evening I was filled with gratitude seeing the pride in my father's eyes and wish I could share the moment with my darling daughter....Today I realize the marathon continues.

An exercise on vulnerability

CHAPTER NINE

PREYING MONSTERS WITH BEADS

(Written February 2023)

When it happened, Samba didn't understand that it was a manifestation of that monster's inner demons. At the time, he was still a virgin and naïve to sexual experiences with girls and boys sitting on other men's laps, holding hands, and other public displays of affection were considered benign throughout society. Men acting on their sexual desires with other men was a completely foreign construct he was yet to be exposed to. But there was a primal discomfort in the hip thrusting and dry humping that was occurring to him. It resulted in a wet stain on the back of his pants, and he didn't fully understand what had just happened until many years later.

The act was never behind closed doors or under the darkness of the night. The act took place in the middle of a neighborhood hangout, where men with lofty aspirations void of any discipline and self-accountability, would waste away their days drinking "Attaya" (Chinese green tea) under a tree. The man was one of the guys, a monster with a sinister smile who always happened to be around young boys, always with his praying beads in hand, and would drop everything to pray as soon as the sound of the Athan (Muslim call for prayer) went off. Samba could not have been his first victim. In hindsight, the society celebrated him as someone who was always there for the kids, often going from neighborhood to neighborhood, household to household on the prowl as a hairy wolf in sheik's clothing masked as everyone's favorite uncle.

Gambian society growing up created an insulated bubble for Samba that kept all-pervasive sexual tendencies of adults, homosexuality, and pedophilia so tucked away in a metaphorical black box, what was meant to be a form of protection turned into extreme exposure and vulnerability of innocent kids with limited intellectual faculties to process molestation in real-time. Most of the time behind each click of praying beads stood preying monsters who had unlimited access to kids soon to be robbed of their sexual innocence.

It was never strangers on the internet searching online platforms for vulnerable kids. It was uncles, aunts, cousins, stepparents, oustasses (Quranic Teachers), and pastors that society's silence was treated as an unspoken green light to hunt at will. In a community where being religious was king and adults never owed an explanation to young children especially when it came to sexuality, compartmentalization became a coping mechanism and a toxic response to trauma.

Who was going to believe Samba?? It could never be mister pious with the praying beads who was everyone's favorite uncle. He could never be a preying monster. It would have taken an attentive parent to notice the silence and confused leer Samba had at the dinner table that evening. The vacancy in his gaze trying to process how an odious erection of a grown adult rubbing against him would alter his perception of all older men he considered as safe spaces. Was this monstrosity a default disposition in all men? He silently wondered. How such a carnal act will forever alter his journey into his sexuality he would never know.

His mother was exhausted from juggling the responsibilities of being a mother of six and a seemingly endless list of household chores. His father, in his customary state of being absent-minded, would seldom direct an intentional gaze at his children to check for any emotional unevenness. However, he mostly remained buried in the newspaper, evening GRTS news on while barking commands from his chair, such as "Make sure all your homework is done, kids! We only get A's in this house! Lawyer! Doctah! Engineer! or Black Sheep!" So, what should have been a moment of reckoning that invoked harsh accountability became yet another insidious act that got locked away in Samba's mind forever.

He was a victim of sexual molestation and perhaps the omnipresent subtlety of the act that never involved exposure and direct manipulations of his private parts, evoking a more visceral reaction made it easy for it to be tucked away until he had a "WAIT A MINUTE! WHAT THE F%&K!! MOMENT" when he was old enough to realize the preying monster with beads that was.

Our country, The Gambia, and by extension, Africa, just like every single country and continent, is flooded with many victims of sexual molestation with varying degrees of severity, some never recover from the trauma. If only walls could talk, what many may have viewed as prayer beads clicking away in the silence of the night would have been exposed as preying monsters with crusty callous hands counting the beads around the bare waist of scared young girls entrusted to family members and friends with sinister sexual deviances.

It is still cringe-worthy when you remember grown adults calling teenage girls "suma jabarr" ("My Wife in Wolof") and making sexual innuendos that wash over responsible adults including parents seeing it as a sign of endearment. So, a whole generation is now old enough to process and unpack all the effects of a society that tolerated the sickness and never held sexual predators accountable. An inherent brokenness in our society's responsibility now impacts scores of marriages and intimate relationships suffering from the consequences of said trauma. Trauma that gets etched as initials with a hot knife onto all baggage being brought into newfound relationships that quality of intimacy oftentimes can dictate reciprocal levels of commitments. How can one unload and articulate all the flashbacks of monsters touching them as children that inject sedating doses of shame and anxiety that can often manifest as a level of asexual coldness from a body's long loss of ability to rid itself of the tense muscles and fretfulness to enjoy uninhibited intimacy?

From women living with a lifetime of shame thinking they were at fault for having the perky breast and plump butts at 14 that enticed their "beloved" 35-year-old uncle, to young boys having bouts of performance anxiety stemming from premature exposure to their neighborhood 45-year-old aunt that always had a transactional warm cookie ready in exchange for much-needed milking and satisfaction from the vigor and prowess of their 15-year-old self that was forced on and into her.

Like Samba, Kumba, Lamin, Fanta, and the many children who have been victims of sexual molestation, society has failed to protect their innocence, and behind many praying beads are preying monsters that have lived among us; some still yet to be held accountable. Their victims are now old enough to display a mature disdain in their looks every time they lay eyes on their monster while still forced by the same society they live in to mask the pain and post-traumatic stress still unpacked.

There are enough silent tears for a nation to perform ablution with. All the times "Maslaha", "Munyal" and "Sutural Ko" (Wolof code words for irrational discretion) have been a default disposition to offer grace to undeserving monsters and have been an intentional middle finger to much-needed healing and reconciliation victims deserve.

Religion has been a saving grace and a beacon of hope for our nation for centuries but when it comes to the worst manifestations of man's ids, severance away from any ideological process of healing is necessary. The recognition of this psychological disposition helps one understand why the default position for most who engage in some of the most heinous acts in African society masks their umbra around a veil of piousness that offers a level of insulation. How could the same protective spiritual structure for the predators designed and often dictated by older men be used as a default prescription to solve ailments of the heart, mind, and body victims of sexual molestation face?

How could the elastic interpretation of Islam by older men who prey upon young women seen fit for marriage and intimacy well before they reach emotional maturity to exercise their agency not be viewed as institutionalized pedophilia? Such conversations can invoke deep levels of discomfort, but no level of piousness should tolerate the sexual advances and exploitation of teenage girls by men old enough for the women to bear their last name not as wives, but as their own children.

Our society has to evolve to a point where the moral character (or lack thereof) of individuals should be examined independently of their perceived piousness and dedication to their method of worship. Any sober person can see right through the BS and fake appearance of righteousness.

Preying monsters living within need the light of day shed on them so their skins burn away like the blood-sucking vampires they are. Our society must also evolve to make conversations around sexuality not taboo. Our children deserve not a brand of protection that keeps them naive. They need to be equipped with tools to identify and communicate any intrusion into their personal space from a sexual standpoint.

Adult men and women preying on young children are pedophiles. Adult men and women engaging in any form of sexual activity or touching are molesters and sexual abusers. For all the victims still harboring scars and suffering in silence. I pray that you never let the stain of your preying monster permeate through you.

Healing takes hardihood but like Samba, the first step is always realizing that the preying monster with beads still and will always harbor the sickness that will haunt him/her forever. For those with children, protect them. Protect them with love. Protect them with information and most importantly pay attention to any discrepancies in their emotional wavelengths especially when palpable displays of unspoken uneasiness happen around preying monsters with beads.

CHAPTER TEN

WHAT'S LOVE GOT TO DO WITH IT?

(Written March 2017)

Samba's Battle

Many in attendance saw in Samba a groom sobbing and barely making it through his vows as the climax of a romantic tale between lovers. The tears were way more than that. That hot day in July was a manifestation of love from his family's presence while also being the most discomfort he had ever felt mentally and emotionally. It felt like an outer body experience. He gazed at his mother as she sat in the front row in search of ardor and affirmation that was just not there. Her face was stoic. Void of expressions beyond fighting grimaces of discomfort. His African father, removed from the emotions of the moment, quietly whispered " You have to be strong" as he saw his son slowly crumble in front of the crowd. The whole experience was foreign and void of a cultural reference point. An

African Muslim family being witness to a traditional American wedding preceded by a Christian pastor in his full garments, forced by the groom to sprinkle verses from both the Quran and Bible in his sermon. Talk about cognitive dissonance.

Part of him felt like he mortgaged a piece of his identity that day. Purged any ounce of political capital African marriages were built on. A framework of cultural norms and safeguards structured to sow seeds of family convergence that were simply never going to be there. He was 25 at the time with little appreciation for how his African identity we're going to be anchored to his ankle. He was with the love of his life and felt their union was going to disrupt those archaic cultural norms of marriage.

Their relationship was built on organic seeds of love, friendship, loyalty and a deep commitment knowing all the moments they navigated an arduous world made them indestructible. "We got us!" they'd often say followed by a Barrack and Michelle fist bump.

His mother, on the other hand, knew and felt something about the journey he was getting ready to embark on. She never lacked love or admiration for the bride, nor was she in utter denial of the union. The idea of marriage in that stage of his life was merely one she felt he was ill-equipped to succeed at nor was it anything she (his mother) had been a product of.

Life around their families was always an interesting dynamic. Samba had assimilated enough into American culture and spending time in the South Side of Chicago with his wife's family was quite natural. The loving environment and nuances of their daily life was one very familiar and made integration quite a natural process. For her it was different. Being around his family was a constant reminder to her that she did not belong. The routine interplay between Wolof (his native tongue) and English alone made spending time with his family an unpleasant experience. " Guys can you please speak English", he often pleaded. She always saw a different version of Samba when he was around family. It was a manifestation of his true self in his comfort zone at a stage in his life when he was yet to define the identity that worked for him. Norms and traditions that were universally understood were ones she lacked understanding and appreciation for. This soon became a source of insecurity for her, assuming she was never going to be "cultured enough" to create that level of comfort for Samba at home. Could you blame her? They both tried forming a union from two very distant points of reference. It soon became apparent especially to Samba that she deserved better. He loved and protected her fiercely so made an effort to limit her exposure to his family and culture, but while doing so, he alienated himself from family bonds he desperately needed to stay grounded.

Samba lived up to the expectations of an unprepared husband. He was selfish, confused and uncomfortable about elements of his cultural identity, insecure about his lack of ability to provide adequately financially and was just lost deep in a journey of self discovery. He was living this married life "dream" in complete contradiction to traditions he grew up seeing and hearing his elders say marriage was indeed about. A marriage that men walked into fully prepared mentally, emotionally and financially to make the marriage be a reflection of their coming to age in society.

In the end, walking away from the marriage was never due to a lack of love and admiration for her. Those feelings never left him. He came to a realization that there was Love and then there was Marriage. The latter had exposed its political complexities to a degree he knew was unsustainable especially when not mature enough to withstand the political pressure of his family's assumption of a fleeting sense of identity.

He had to embark on a journey of self discovery, alone.

Samba's long road to redemption

Being married and divorced before 30 had sent him through waves of trying to make sense of "Love" as we know it while balancing the political and rational elements, he knew dictated the success of any future marriage. What seemed apparent to him was that being attracted to and developing emotional bonds with women was never the problem. After his divorce, he dated, "talked to," and had interest in some amazing women who were queens in their own right. He was emotionally scarred from having loved and received love from an organic place yet found it unable to withstand external pressures. They were just never in a place to conceptualize the quest he was on when out of the blue, became the guy who gracefully bowed out. Many of them saw this as a cold, selfish and misleading act of betrayal which was fair. He saw it as avoiding the inevitability of not being the version of the man they wanted and the dynamic of not being one that created political harmony within his family. He had once loved in the purest form that didn't yield the peace of mind he deserved. He therefore saw every ounce of emotional and aspirational capital some women invested in him as one that hindered them from making rational and political decisions of their own to give access to another man worthy of them.

Samba's story is one of many among first-generation Americans and African immigrants in the diaspora. Stuck between two worlds trying to organically breed hybrid relationships with enough commonality to satisfy particular traditions and cultural norms latched on to us to serve as anchors.

To understand such complexities, one must dig deeper into two very elusive concepts.

Love and Marriage: Kumba Banjul, Samba Banjul

Before the indoctrination of western ideas of romance, Marriage was merely a political arrangement family made within the confines of social class, tradition, and religion. An institution built not around the "love" two eventual couples had for each other but the importance of maintaining family status and formidability within society.

For example, in Africa, arranged marriages were not only predominant but also necessary to maintain a particular order in the social hierarchy. Males lived their young lives building up clout as formidable men and providers, while the females were sheltered as much as possible to present the most refined version of a virgin woman worthy of the most significant dowry (bride prize). As a man, the more wealth you had, the more wives and children you had. Wives lived in harmony mostly caring for all the children irrespective of whose womb they came out of. The idea of Love was communal.

Growing up in The Gambia, Samba was not far removed from such a dynamic either. Many of his grandfathers and uncles had multiple wives. Not only did it speak to their status in society, but it was also accepted in his Islamic religion. This was very confusing to him at first because part of his ratiocinative associations about marriage were greatly influenced by the recent agreements of marriage. "How could a man love more than one woman equally?" He would question. "I thought marriage was a sacred union between one man and one woman? Whatever happened to "his rib?" The fusion of souls that oozed love and romance. You know, the Romeo and Juliet " You die, I die" kind of love. Wouldn't the act of courting a potential second wife be the textbook definition of modern-day cheating?

If Islam said you can have four, but Christianity said (eventually) only one. Who was right and who was wrong? Polygamy (or more accurately polygyny) was justified in Islam from the premise of the man's ability to feed, clothe and satisfy women in bed under the condition that he treated them equally. It made sense from a numbers standpoint. Women always outnumbered men throughout history. More men died in combat during ancient wars leaving widows behind, female babies turned out more resilient to withstand infant mortality rates versus male babies, and in cases of infertility in women, polygyny still gave a man a chance to bear kids and continue his legacy. There were also the more crude acts of brutality that existed in cultures that killed off their female babies because only a son was deemed worthy. The accumulation of all these factors made sense for a man to be able to marry multiple wives and provide security for more than one woman. It also strengthened his political powers freeing families of the burden of caring for a woman who is of age.

Even in Christianity, monogamy was something that was agreed on by church leaders and embedded in biblical doctrine as a sacred union between man and woman. Very little explicit condemnations of polygamy existed in the old testament. The idea of "Love" as a prerequisite for marriage was a foreign and sometimes deemed foolish concept concerning social norms. The love grew from the union as a by-product of sustained companionship, sexual intimacy, and friendship. Going back further to our hunter and gathering days even reveal the level of political and rational calibrations that went into choosing a mate. Women positioned themselves to "Alpha males" with aims of securing basic needs of food, shelter, and protection.

So when did the switch happen?? When did marriage become synonymous with love or be based on love being the prerequisite and not the by-product of a sound, rational and political decision? When did married couples start expecting a level of fulfillment and sustained emotional bliss from their partners? A dynamic that shunned social diversification of needs and individuality. Falling in love, dating/courting, being engaged and married has gradually evolved to significant others living years under strict confines of exclusivity in interactions that render them extremely lonely as soon as the relationship ends or a partner dies. The whole soulmate concept from a logical standpoint alone is quite peculiar, to say the least, but is undoubtedly a foreign concept in the history of marriages between humans. Most people tend not to be married to the love of their life due to one reason or another.

Samba's mother's favorite saying as they got older and started navigating romantic relationships was " Kumba Banjul, Samba Banjul." A Wolof saying that meant you marry someone who is cut from the same moral and cultural cloth as you were. They knew who you were, what you were not and most importantly shared the same cultural reference of what marriage was about. She was never easily impressed with the high school and college sweethearts he would come home drunk in love over. "Love's got nothing to do with finding a wife, boy" she would always say. She not only felt "Love" indeed made him dumb and deaf but also ultimately, rationality, not emotions dictated the quality of life good partnership brought.

He saw more into the "Kumba Banjul, Samba Banjul" saying. " Kumba", the female, came first in the reference. An inference establishing her agency in the union. Growing up at home he never considered his dad a "romantic" guy in the modern sense of romance. The "bringing flowers home" "baby, I love you" kind of way. Frankly, all five kids would die of laughter if their dad walked into the house crooning "baby, I love you" to their mom. She, on the other hand, was very measured with her public displays of affection towards their dad in front of them. There was never the "here's your warm plate, daddy and let me rub your tummy afterward." That version of "Love" just did not radiate through Samba's household. Mom's love was always channeled from a position of strength and never a place of submission.

Samba never once questioned the existence of love between his parents and saw it manifested invariably in more meaningful ways. He saw it in the way his father spoke about his mother and the reverence he had in her level of beauty, independence and grace. He revered her agency and never gave any slight inclination of unequal governance of house matters. Polygyny was all around Samba's father, and he had the social status that was often a precursor to wife number two. The possibility never crossed his mind because he knew and saw the devotion his dad had for their partnership.

Samba's mom was the epitome of a woman with agency. She came from a lineage of empowered women and was a living embodiment of it. Women that never aspired just to be a "better half" but a wholesome and able "plus one." She indeed was a wonder woman in his eyes. A woman filled with poise and grace, accompanied with a level of quarantined ferocity that none of the kids wanted any part of. She created a transformative ecosystem where both mom and dad were formidable sources of love, provision, and oversight. She stood tall (actually taller) and proud to be a queen right next to his dad. To this day, she maintains a superior level of emotional intelligence and knack for knowing just the right type and amount of love her husband and all her five kids need.

Samba would have been naive to assume their marriage was perfect either. Name one that is. He was sure the union faced numerous trials most of which he frankly never wished to know. He felt like they found a way to work it out without any casualties of emotional poison injected into the kids. They sustained a healthy dynamic that shaped all their lives. His sisters were never destined to be women yearning for a well to do man to rescue them in marriage but also women of agency. The men, on the other hand, grew up to have no desire for a woman who did not stand independently on her own.

When it came to love though, Samba had given up on the idea of finding or seeking it as the foundation of a sustainable marriage dynamic—if what he once felt wasn't great enough to overcome the cultural interference, no other similar potency was possible to create.

A sad disposition one would say but perhaps time, growth and coming of age as an independent man would allow him to captain the truest desires of his heart, mind and soul void of any mental shackles.

CODA (Reflection on Samba's Experience)

So, what's love got to do with Marriage??

Everything? Nothing at all? At what stage?? I really do not know.

What can I know at 32? I have been wrong so many times about love and marriage that I find delight in exploring my blind spots in retrospect. Amazed at how I was able to feel so strongly about someone or an idea of a relationship just for those feelings to lack the fortitude to overcome the reality of culture and political interference in marriage. I've lived through, been a product of, and identify culturally (religion and tradition), with so many versions of marriage to realize only an individual can determine what works for them. What influences their approach to love and marriage?

In the words of Kanye, "YOU AIN'T GOT THE ANSWERS, SWAY!!"

Everyone is entitled to their own truth. I can only see things through a lens shaded by my personal experiences.

At some point in my life, I harbored a sense of resentment towards traditional African parents and families always hovering over the decision making of who to marry yet are sometimes nowhere to provide comfort in lonely moments of despair managing a heart aching for love that was once so familiar and unadulterated.

One thing is for certain, like Samba, everyone at a point in their life deserves to have felt love in its purest form, irrespective of all the other complexities that can come with the other stuff.

CHAPTER ELEVEN

P.S I LOVE YOU, MAN

(Written December 2018)

Part 2: What's Love got to do with it?

It always puzzled Samba how unnatural the words *"I love you"* felt coming out of his mouth growing up. This queasy, foreign and hazy declaration that was meant to stem from a deep yearning to fulfill the emotional and physical needs of a partner, family member or friend. He had grown up mostly seeing "love" manifested only as a prelude to a romantic affair. A fickle pronouncement that soon became a faux confirmation or prognosis of a relationship and its potential. A routine utilization of the word that slowly evolved into a casual end to phone conversations and text messages; *"ok TTYL babes, I love you..."* mostly void of any layered meaning or conviction.

He was not an outlier in such a narrow and binary expression and understanding of love either. Majority of his society growing up operated on those terms. As a man, you loved your mother dearly as the first recognition of the concept that contoured the cognitive disposition of the love you desired. The second type of love was the one you spoke of only concerning romantic affairs. Affairs often measured in the man's ability to *"Werrseh"* (*A Wolof term for showering love interests with gifts and money).* Love was mostly only seen, received and sought after through the permeable emotional membrane of a man and a woman. A dynamic that almost excluded the role fathers played in this construct void of masculine osmosis.

Why were African men almost entirely excluded from the organic manufacturing of their young boy's emotional capacities? Why did boys live a lifetime of youth without ever hearing the words *"I love you, son"* uttered from their father? Was it a genetic coding they also lacked from a patriarchal lineage of emotional deficiency? Why such an inherent callous and sexist *"feelings are for gals' '* approach society took to raising men? An intentional lack of emotional attention that cultivated a brand of toxic masculinity that turned many blind to the importance of such a facet of intelligence and well being crucial for their vitality.

Too much expression of emotions and feelings of vulnerability was considered a sign of weakness in a man. A concept so unconventional; it did not exist in the lexicon of many local languages. The few flashes of attention tended not to be of the soothing, comforting type but of the " *you are a warrior, and big boys don't wince or cry out loud"* brand. " *Son, you have to be strong"* being a translation for *"I'm sorry you're hurting"* or *"Things will get better".*

Father's in the community mortgaged away almost every aspect of young men's development. When it came to faith and learning about God, the *"Oustass"* (Quranic teacher) was responsible for that. A rigorous but nebulous delivery of the religion to most young men that came from a vantage point of fearing Allah's punishment than it did being a gentle extension of God's love.

When it came to sports or physical activity, *"boy, you better not let your grades slip from all that goofing around with games"* was a more common predisposition than pops in the stands waiting to give you feedback on your defensive errors on the way to grab ice cream cones.

Young boys mostly learned from observations about what love was supposed to be like and received societal reassurance that being educated and with a job to provide for a woman (or women) were merely the threshold to securing "love".

Boys therefore transitioned to men with a primitive understanding of how to tend to their emotions and be held accountable by their fellow men.

A father to son emotional outlet was seldom open to address any vulnerabilities. Missing a brand of love that was strong but gentle and nuanced. A type of love that cultivated an inclination for the intangible gestures (ie. quality time and a listening ear) that meant way more than an expensive Louis Vuitton purse.

Samba observed the dynamic of his African culture and saw the root cause of his battles with receiving and giving love. Majority of the manifestations of love around him hinged on a man's ability to provide. As a young adult, he consequently felt insecure and inadequate in love not being able to provide for the people he loved. He grew distant and isolated from any loved one he had nothing tangible to offer. How could you blame his insecurity? Being a formidable provider was paramount in his culture. Transitioning to a higher economic status in society gave men a sense of power and invisibility with society creating a buffer for any abuse of said acidic power.

He observed countless older men and women inculcate in their daughters the mindset of *"Munyalal sa sohla rek"* (*Wollof saying that means one being more compromising and patient in a difficult situation knowing a better circumstance elsewhere was not guaranteed*).

The young women were being trained to mortgage away their agency, live through unhealthy relationships and accept mediocrity in men who sought after them lazily in love just because they portrayed a level of financial security all parents prayed for their daughters.

"Munyalal sa sohla rek" became the permanent state that steadily graded men on a curve perpetuating a toxic conundrum of sexism and predisposition to abuse. Society was telling Samba every single day that so long as he met meek standards of provision, there was always a household willing to offer their daughter's agency in marriage.

There was always a *"Munyalal sa sohla"* at the doorsteps of every foul and abusive act from men. An abyss of unbecoming men who had no incentive to be emotionally invested in the lives of their wives and children.

Men physically and verbally abusing their wives... *"but did you see the car he bought her last year?"*

Men working all day, coming home briefly for lunch, and back out to rendezvous with friends missing every little nuance of attention their young children may have needed from their father... *"but did you see the new house he is building for them?"*

Men leaving a wife and two kids to marry a new wife the age of their oldest daughter......*"But don't you see he is still sending money to them? Plus, she does not have to work!"*

The whispers, cries and scars of women slowly drowned by the echoes of enabling bystanders in society giving hollow assurances that simply rang the same melancholic tune..."*Munyalal sa sohla*".

Love, seen only through the lens of provision, gave men no incentive to address the epidemic that was their lack of advanced emotional capacities to meet the sophistication of female counterparts that genuinely deserved better.

Gender-based violence runs rampant in a society rotting from its unwillingness to acknowledge and dismantle patriarchal systems that fail to hold men accountable for violence against women.

Samba realized he was part of the problem and a product of it. He learned more about his emotional disposition around the idea of "Love" at the expense of many who loved and cared for him through his adulthood.

Living in America demanded a level of emotional presence and engagement in relationships more than was ever required back home. One that forced him to verbalize his feelings without running the risk of losing his Jola warrior card. Love meant something entirely different to him at 11 than it did at 21 and now at 31. An ability to provide was amicable and made partnership easy but was not an emotionally exclusive disposition coming from a culture that wealth gave way to freedom to "provide" for as many women as possible.

Coda...

Samba's dilemma and observations speak to a more significant problem affecting African societies. In the deep-layered history of our patriarchal and sexist past lies a nagging avoidance of men investing in the emotional upbringing of their sons. Our entire marital system is based not on scrutinizing the content of a man's character and emotional well being first but rather the size of his dowry and the sustainability of his economic vitality. It's one of the many side effects of an impoverished society that perhaps force the downtrodden to make or influence decisions out of desperation. However, a sliver of hope does exist with fortunes of our women changing through higher education and respectable economic status in society earned independent of a "rich" husband. Valor and vulnerability are slowly infiltrating the current generation of men ready to break down the walls of masculine recoil.

Love is nothing but one of many manifestations of human emotion. Like any emotion, it requires proper nurturing to understand and experience its potency fully. Understanding that must come from teachings from our parents on how to harness the emotion to help enrich our lives.

My experiences are based on living in Gambian society, and I yearn for days where fathers are more emotionally involved and present in the lives of their sons especially. I genuinely believe if young boys heard " *I love you"* from the men in their lives, it will enrich their emotional dimensions and understanding of Love with its accompanying complexities.

There is a powerful unclenching effect in verbalizing those three words of affirmation. It can tame a propensity for disruptive, outward or physical expressions of unattended hurt or confusion. It can make young men more responsive to the tactile stimulations of the human experiences around them.

Our sisters and daughters are growing up in a world where their men lack emotional sophistication required to match their undying loyalty. But for how long? At what cost?

Kumba Banjul, Samba Banjul sounds good and all but at some point, Kumba Banjul, Samba Brooklyn is a better option, and Kumba should not hesitate at all!

CHAPTER TWELVE

MY TRUE NORTH

(Written June 2022)

The birth of my daughter, Isha Haddy, nearly four years ago on September 22nd, 2018, will always be the day my heart was awakened to feel and receive a brand of love that was truly unconditional. An overwhelming first step into a journey of fatherhood that would forever change how I see the world.

I find it quite odd that prior to our ultrasound visit months into our pregnancy, I had never conceptualized life with a daughter. Not sure if it's society's way of programming men to seek that flawed narrative of "young Simba" who grows up to be king, but here I was grappling with the news of being a newly minted #GirlDad!

A revelation that was as exciting as it was filled with anxiety. She would not come with an instruction manual and I knew deep down, new layers of vulnerability were to be exposed in a way I had never experienced.

Fast forward to present-day Isha Haddy giving her first public speech at the age of three, being an encapsulation of the wonderful journey of fatherhood I have been on since her birth. The past years have provided steady doses of black girl magic, watching her blossom with varying strokes of brilliance and idiosyncrasy, familiar to both her mother and me. *(She still is a copy-paste version of me!)*

Every iteration of her growth and development since birth has infused me with joy which I could not have imagined. Her intuitiveness, curiosity, wit, and sense of humor constantly serve as pure oxygen in my life.

A muse she has truly become - fiddling with all the strings of my heart to a spiritual tune no woman has ever been able to amplify.

The backdrop of the journey, however, has also been filled with intermittent doses of guilt and sorrow considering the crazy turn in my life attending to another child *(my budding start-up business Innovarx)* that has robbed me of so many nights when I couldn't hold her and read bedtime stories to the love of my life.

Balancing the polar extremes of pure bliss and emotional guilt has defined so much of my experience as a father. A rollercoaster many adults experience as they become fathers while balancing the raging demands of a professional career, often designed to disrupt all aspects of work-life balance.

Beneath my tall frame lies minefields of insecurity, anxiety, and vulnerability, with the daily price she pays because of my ambition. The impatience with my work now, I've realized, is a constant race against the calcification of her memories of me being constantly away. I'll always wish I could get some moments of her infancy back, but a reorientation of my compass would not have happened without the pain absence has caused.

Fatherhood has also given me whole new respect for mothers seeing the physical, mental and emotional sacrifice her mother (Adama) makes daily to maintain her sustenance. I remember vividly seeing my wife's strength shine through 18 hours of labor, thinking no superficial layers of my muscular frame could ever match her sinew.

I would have died!

No wonder most African men traditionally stay out of the delivery room *(my father included)*. I think witnessing a woman sacrifice her body to bring a child into this world should forever calibrate the required level of adoration and respect she deserves for the rest of her existence.

I could never repay my wife Adama for the heaven-sent gift Isha Haddy is to me.

Even after birth, there's little credit I can take for Isha's growth to date, knowing the level of grace and patience Adama has afforded me over the past few years. I've spent more nights on the road chasing my dream than at home with them.

This unsettling reality has always been symbolic of generations of absentee fatherhood that have plagued our family line. A disposition acceptable in a society that glorifies the tale of the ambitious and courageous man always returning home with depleted energy stores incapable of tilling the emotional soils of their children.

A by-product of my relationship with my daughter has consequently been deep introspection about my relationship with my father. Taking inventory of the facets of our relationship that shaped the man I am today.

The irony of my relationship with my father is that all the moments spent away from Isha Haddy over the past two years have been extended periods with him being back at home *(Gambia)*, where he is now retired after a long career. I often say we are getting to know each other for the first time in our lives *(at 36 and 71 years old respectively)* and, to a certain extent, it is true.

My Father, like many African fathers in his generation, saw fatherhood only through the lens of provision and discipline. Often mortgaging away the tactile requirements of nurturing to exhausted mothers often caught rationing out love and attention to multiple children with varying needs.

As an adult, being able to unpack the effects of such a dynamic between a father and child that felt more like a professional autocratic relationship has left me with many undesirable aspects I choose not to incorporate into my fatherhood toolbox.

I had a father whose love language from day one was ambition and achievement. And boy, did he inject it into my veins. I attribute so much of my confidence and self-belief to his priming and psychological programming, even if the package came with side effects of him not being in tune with my emotions and vulnerabilities.

Being the middle child of five kids, I, therefore, grew up with thoughts and views divergent from what was considered family doctrine mandated by my father. I was the rebel in the house who was most emotionally independent and forced my way to dance to my beat even at the cost of the usual beatings and disciplinary actions of my dad.

Like me, my father was dedicated to his career in a way that left little time for conversations around topics that had no predetermined dominant voice. I don't recall having any deep conversations about love, financial literacy, wealth creation, spirituality, sex, or any pressing matter that called for democratized engagement. He was intermittently present in mind and attention, even if his lingering expectations of what we were to become hovered over us from Alaska to Johannesburg.

Growing up, it was quite normal that dad was always away at work, sometimes in another country. Society always gave an excuse to fathers not being present in the day-to-day lives of their kids as long as their status in society and jobs provided ample "security" and a constant roof over the heads of their children.

Unpacking the effects of a long-desired exploration of who he is and him knowing who I was as a child and now adult initially came with a bit of resentment.

I journeyed so much of my life without him really knowing my real-time mental and emotional calibrations, but how could I demand such emotional intelligence from a man born into a polygamous family and who lost his own father when he was only 10 years old?

His story as a child is filled with tragedy, being the victim of all the complexities of an ominous, patriarchal African polygamous family.

He never had the tools to lean into fatherhood with confidence, knowing which levers to push and pull to create wholesome relationships with all his kids at a deep emotional level. He overachieved in the fatherhood department, knowing none of us at any point felt like we lacked loved and protection from him.

Ultimately, any father's capacity is often influenced by their experience as a son and in that regard, my father accomplished a tremendous feat when compared to his father. I think the demands of fatherhood have evolved from an era where provision and protection reign supreme over what was deemed fickle needs for constant emotional involvement.

Now, as two adults, our intergenerational conversations have evolved into heated dinner table banter between men who see the world differently sometimes.

I've grown to ask him hard questions about his life to help make sense of mine. Stories about his relationship with his dad *(and family)* that, for decades, had been hidden in the repository of discomfort reveal a level of emotional fortitude that allowed him to navigate all the storms in his life.

Grace and understanding of all the trauma the void of an active father left in him has allowed me to shape my relationship with my daughter and finally start breaking some of the generational cycles. Putting in intentional efforts and strategies to improve on the design, he handed over to me. A complete 2018 fatherhood software update from his 1985 version.

The fact that I end every conversation with my daughter by verbally telling her "I Love You" is earth-shattering innovation in fatherhood in my family. Three potent words that have an reprieving and cathartic effect most children growing up in African homes never had the privilege of hearing.

My relationship with my father has now developed into a fraternal type of love where we both have a level of agency in our thoughts and can express them freely. I embody so many of his gifts and traits that there's always a subconscious acknowledgement of our inherent nature. I have grown to love him for who he is and have never felt the absence of his steadfast love and support.

Curiosity has guided my relationship with my daughter ever since she was born. Every day brings new questions and observations about her surroundings that I am so eager to learn. Ask her how she feels and thinks about everything to make her realize it is in questioning the oddities of life that knowledge and wisdom are found.

I cannot wait to have deep conversations about faith and religion with her. Make her understand that spirituality *(which was born in her)* will and should always be the guiding principle in her life *(not religion)*. Guard her mind against the narration of God's love for us humans from a perspective of a man's dominance and female submission as told by many religious texts.

Her being raised Muslim is of importance but simply as a foundation of her faith and a viable avenue for cultivating an individual relationship with God that will breed wholesome virtues of good moral character in her.

I hope that as she grows and attains maturity in her intellectual and logical faculties, she will have the pluck to explore and read scriptures from Christianity, Hinduism, Buddhism, and traditional African religions to find the common thread of grace, love (not fear), and protection from a higher power in them all. Spiritual gateways to discovering the God inside of her.

I cannot wait to have conversations about the love and betrayal she is bound to experience especially after having my unconditional love as a benchmark that will shape the quality of steadfast love she will seek in other men programmed from birth with the privilege of always having agency in choice.

I wonder sometimes how I could guard her against the different seasons of heartbreak she is bound to face, but am certain that her cup of love will always be so full leaving the house, it will serve as an invisible cloak to weather all storms. She will never have an iota of doubt that she is loved beyond ever needing another man to validate her worthiness. I will, still need to convince her to rid herself of the western notion of taking another man's last name!

I cannot wait to have a conversation about the need to not do extraordinary things in life as a way of receiving love and approval from me. I will be a safety net guarded trampoline that allows her to fall and be propelled back up into the sky. That emotional pit stop that allows her to acknowledge the weariness of life she will have to navigate alone sometimes.

So much of the urgency to attain financial freedom in our life right now (as parents) is geared towards allowing her to choose her path in life from a place of seeking fulfillment in a life of purpose and not from a place of desperation.

Being "Born Again" is often a term referring to a moment of awakening and renewing one's dedication to God, but being Isha's father has been nothing short of a spiritual awakening for me.

Being a father of a daughter has exposed me to how unbalanced and often neglecting the world, our African societies and families, are to the plight of a woman. Especially a Black woman.

A world where women's agency to choose and define life on their terms is still held captive by the stranglehold of patriarchy and toxic masculinity.

I etched her name with ink on my shoulder when she was born because for the first time in my life; I knew there was a commitment to love and protection that was forever going to be non-negotiable.

Isha Haddy has become my true north and has affected and influenced every decision in my life since the day she was born.

Sometimes I feel like she is growing up to have an uncanny radar for my emotional dispositions to know when exactly to provide a warm embrace that dissipates all my worries into thin air.

The therapeutic effects of her smile and warm gaze being something I yearn for knowing I will always be a hero in her eyes.

I love her more than life itself and my greatest ambition will always be for Isha to grow to know my authentic self, not as the world may see me, but just as her perfectly imperfect father.

A father who, through the gift of a daughter and manifestations of a version of myself born again through her, has a second chance at erasing all the pitfalls of fatherhood from generations past.

So, to all my fathers out there, especially my dad and older brother Malick,

Happy Father's Day!

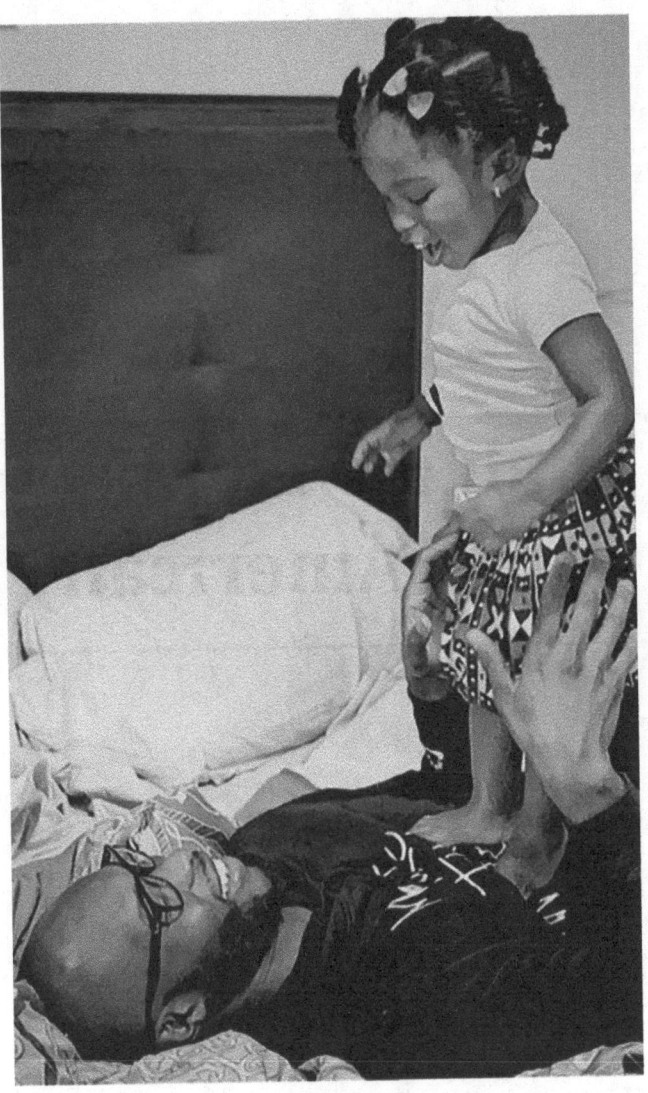

Assuming the role of trampoline as a feature of my first days back home after being away for months in The Gambia. Rekindling all the bonds with my muse.

Call me Ishmail (I am American)

CHAPTER THIRTEEN

HELLO COUSIN

(Written August 2019)

Dearest Cousin

As I stare at the Atlantic Ocean waves splash against the shores of the smiling coast, I call home; her spiritual magnificence resonates deeply within me. The might of her every tide manifesting a presence of both calmness and rage in its expression. A mythical display of duality symbolic of all the hidden stories about our people we may never know. Thousands of our ancestors' souls occupy the depths of her being and embody experiences of a middle passage that forever changed our shared history.

A reflection of a history that makes me wonder what happened, Cousin?

Why was I raised with little to no stories about who you were?

Why do we refer to Ancestors stolen from our lands as "Yours and Ours"?

Cousin, why were you raised to know so little about who I was?

What went wrong? Who made it go wrong?

I thought the family was meant to stick together?

See, Cousin, for so long, all we knew about you and our family across the pond were cultural presentations a few of us that consumed American media received. Our idea of people who looked like us but lived in "Cannah Land" was a strategically packaged idiom that always came with more swag than substance. Conduits of the Black American culture that wore hoop earrings and basketball shorts, glitter jackets with jerry curls, not black leather jackets with black leather gloves. It gave us ideas on how we wanted to dance, dribble, and mime. A passport to finesse a three-month holiday in "Yankee land" into an unchallenged right to twist English language into as much slang as possible. Our talent shows featured "P-Diddy" and "Bad-Boy" Harlem shakes not re-enactments of James Weldon Johnson poems from the Harlem Renaissance era. Langston WHOOO???

The version of history we learned in school was void of any acknowledgment of the beautiful matrix that is our shared history. A system that turned figures like Nat Turner into a ghost that never existed in our history books. Till this day, more people on the continent know about Emmitt Smith than they do Emmett Till as if beatings on black bodies have not been a spectator sport for centuries now. Our ignorance of the trauma that happened beyond the "door of no return" 400 years ago turned us into the way we are, Cousin.

Being born in Africa doesn't make us any more T'Challa than Killmonger. Truth is, most millennial Africans choose to omit the fact that we are just as clueless about Africa as our brethren in the diaspora.

Some of our exposure to different African cultures happen outside of the continent, specifically in the U.S. or Europe when we are bonded by association. Yes, we have African customs that we appreciate and may have experienced, but we have very little attachment and commitment to passing them along to our kids born away from the continent and undergo almost total assimilation into western life. We consider many traditional teachings of medicine and superstitions to be primitive and unbecoming.

Most first-generation African kids today may have a closet full of traditional garments, African names but do not speak the native languages nor can they articulate the origin and traits of their cultural heritage.

My unfiltered enlightenment about the history of descendants of enslaved Africans living in the Americas made me realize how blind the motherland has been to their plight. The assumption that slavery was horrible, but it ended, and life soon became "MTV Cribs" and "Pimp my ride" was so far from the truth.

See, cousin, the pages missing in the texts were the most important ones. The real history about the race being far from attaining the freedom "all men" were promised by the nation's founding fathers after slavery was forced to an end. America has been chasing after the realization of said promise for centuries now. Eras of reconstruction, ushering in Jim Crow laws, and quest for civil rights, all have their remnants entrenched in society with mass incarceration, school segregation, voter suppression still used as tools of disenfranchisement. Systems that make it almost impossible to actualize full agency and close the wealth gap that utilized a 400-year head start as rocket fuel. Many Africans that immigrated to America fail to respect and reconcile with this sobering reality. Making it to the land of "milk and honey" in search of greener pastures gave way to immediately reaping the benefits of all the progress made and become just as viable to fill any corporate minority quota.

So I know the shock of the world to injustices and systems of oppression being more visible under the current polarized state of affairs feels like a slap in the face. Your pain and trauma have always been elements the world assigned magical powers to numb out, forgive and forget. The discussion of its depth and complexity causes too much discomfort and rage.

I, therefore, write to you from a deep place of sorrow, disappointment, and guilt knowing for so long our elders failed to retain the penmanship of our family history. It should not have taken me living in America to fully educate myself about the shared history of our people. We lost the battle in the version of history turned into doctrine. Our ancestors' affinity to oral history delivered under the baobab tree blinding them to the wave of mass programming slavery, imperialism, and colonialism brought. We tried so hard to remain as *Simba* in the story, knowing very well that any story told by the hunter, never favored the lion.

Cousin, our educational systems in Africa are rigorously designed to prepare us for our mass exodus to the U.S and Europe. The end goal is to continue building those great nations with our intellectual might not to return home to build our continent. Makes you wonder if the slave-trade ever ended? Or did it morph from physical to intellectual bondage? Went from submission by capture to volunteer exodus of the brightest from the continent. What is left behind? The poor who cannot afford migration are ruled by corrupt leaders that serve as obedient dogs to western leaders while using the natural resources to enrich themselves.

Ask any Black person under 40 born in Africa to tell you where they are from and wait for the answer. I, for one, will tell you with pride that I am Gambian. Ask me to tell you more and I will specifically tell you I identify as Jola by virtue of my last name and heritage but was raised Wolof due to the strong influence of my mother's heritage.

My Lineage. My paternal grandparents hailed from the Jola and Mandinka people, while my maternal grandparents of Wolof and Serer extraction. I learned how to speak Wolof when my family moved back to The Gambia and can also hold a conversation in Mandinka. My accent is a byproduct of a constant interchange between English (my first language) and Wolof (my second).

The Jola people are one of the smallest ethnic groups in the Senegambia region and, unlike other Senegambian ethnic groups, they do not have a caste system or social structure of nobles, slaves, griots, etc. I find great pride in that attribute and try to maintain that ethos today. They are hardworking and industrious people who migrated from parts of southern Egypt via present day Burkina Faso, Guinea Bissau, Senegal and The Gambia bringing palm-seed, cotton, and rice with them. They also were some of the last tribes in the region to accept Islam and Christianity. They were great warriors and were hired as mercenaries during religious wars like the Soninke-Marabout wars in the 1800s.

I never met my dad's father, Mankamang Badjie. He was a Jola warrior from Kankurang, Bwiam, a confidant of the rulers of Fulladu (Alpha Molloh Bandeh and Musa Molloh Bandeh) sent to create a new settlement in the Upper Fulladu West region—Bansang to be specific.. Grandpa Mankamang had four wives and over a dozen children. Bansang soon became a melting pot of cultures with Mandinkas, Jolas, Fulas and other tribes living in harmony. His legacy of strength, gallantry, and sense of community lives in me today even though his folklore is that of a fictional Wakandan character to me. He would undoubtedly be the first superhero my children will learn about.

Ask me to tell you more and boy the story starts to get fuzzy....

The fact that most Africans today identify first with a country tells you all you need to know about how far removed from our true heritage we are and the number colonialism did on us.

Being born in what is called "The Gambia" is meaningless in the context of who I truly am. Africa as we know it today is simply a post-colonial dissection based on European allocations of natural resources and has nothing to do with the people. I don't have to trace back two back to two generations to see the shift in migration that happened in my family from Senegal, Guinea Bissau ending up in The Gambia.

Dearest Cousin

I understand.

I do not blame you for how you also treated me as a stranger from a foreign land where people ran naked with giraffes and lived in trees. All those *"African booty scratcher"* jokes stung the most coming from you. I was once one of those kids my kindergarten teacher painted a picture of our homeland that left me feeling more like *Curious George* than curious about *George Washington Carver*. I had to return home to rewire my brain to see the beauty in the continent and establish a sense of pride. The system of western education was strategically designed to keep the riches of *Mansa Musa* as hidden as the richest nations in the west amassed on the backs of our ancestors. *Timbuktu* was never going to make it into an American history book or two when HIS-story was to maintain the bottom-up narrative of our civilization. History told that began in a physically captive state was to shackle our minds in a state of transitioning from needing salvation to being "given" salvation by the same group of people. Lost in the adulterated history presented was our rich culture, language, identity, sense of pride and ownership in a home that soon became foreign. An Africa that was a beautiful tapestry of 1.2 billion kings and queens traded in for a mindset of being a labeled "minority" in a land barely one-fourth the size of the motherland.

Our version of Wakanda did exist on the continent! Intellectual ingenuity was the bedrock of civilizations. Spirituality is woven in each tribes' DNA irrespective of their form of expression. Neither Islam nor Christianity was ever needed for the higher power to reign his grace over the motherland. Politics and economic restructuring brought "religion" to the Africans not a lack of connection to God. To this day, a confusing dichotomy exists with Africans claiming a major religion with a side of the good ole "Marabout" / Voodoo man who sees and heals "all things". The fact that we celebrate "Independence Day" post colonization in itself is ironic. It's nothing more than celebrating conformity to a western way of governance that is built on a level of intellectual and economic supplication.

The awkwardness that therefore existed when we first started to know each other was a reflection of the division sowed by the selective commentary of our history. The idea that "Africans also sold their fellow brothers and sisters" still woven in the final cut of narration despite massive omissions meant to attenuate the acidity of the cruelty. A cunning way of using a brush broad enough for its strokes to illustrate gray areas on an ugly portrait of humanity. A canvas that attempted to associate the roots of such cruelty in human transactions and not an ideology that Black people were less than with bodies built for servitude even in the eyes of God.

Dearest Cousin...

Where do we go from here? Wettin man go do!? What do the next 400 years hold for us, cousin? What layers would our generation seek to add as we seize the captainship of our joint destiny? We must seek the truth ourselves from each other before any proper reconciliation can happen. No longer can we blame anyone for not knowing what we don't know about each other.

You may feel the sorrow of being taken away from your homeland, but truth be told, we have not held up our end of the bargain with keeping our house in order. Everyone but us sees her unlimited potential and reaping the best of what Mama Africa has to offer. The independence our forebears fought and died for has yet to be willed into existence. Poverty is still rife and prosperity yet to be actualized. Most of us could not even conceptualize true prosperity until a fictional Wakanda was presented to us.

The elephant in the room has also always been the unspoken tension between some Africans on the continent and their brethren in the diaspora. Who is more authentic? Who is the "lost child"?. The mental constructs run so deep that Africans on the continent who may be unexposed only see Black Americans in the light of entertainers (Athletes and Rappers) or "lazy people" squandering golden opportunities. Being "urban or hip" in an African sense weighs heavily on one's level of cultural appropriation of Hip-hop culture.

Then you have the flip side of African Americans who may be unexposed/uninformed only viewing "The Country Africa" as a shithole (his words not mine) jungle unworthy of reestablishing any connection and seeing African immigrants as less than polished individuals. A sense of identity linked to the nation of birth rather than the origin of their ancestors. African Americans constitute some of the richest Black people in the world yet rarely invest in business and economic opportunities in Africa.

"The fierce urgency of now." There is an urgency for us all to return for fellowship under the baobab tree. Sow new seeds of hope and start using the motherland as the omnipotent source of power she is for all her children around the world.

A change in narrative and re-wiring of our perceptions of each other is desperately needed. As a people, we have spent so much time going against each other and highlighting what makes us different while our continent, rich in heritage and history, is decaying in front of our eyes.

Homecoming: our ancestors' wildest dreams beckon. "Home" is subjective and truly lies where one's heart is. Our continent needs rejuvenation as it becomes the next frontier for innovation and economic expansion. Its transformations are inevitable, but the drivers of a said revolution who will reap its benefits are yet to be determined.

As noted above, it is undeniable that the richest Black people with the most economical power live in America yet very few think Africa when it comes to investments, innovation, and job creation. With Africa's population expected to balloon up to 2.5 billion people by 2050, there is not a single trade or skill void of potential to be monetized on the continent. To fully manifest into our ancestors wildest dreams, our talents, ingenuity, and resources must start permeating back into the continent.

I dream of the day we all find a place on the continent to call our home. A day where our African leaders see value in creating an atmosphere conducive to a homecoming that includes a claim to citizenship of any nation, one traces back their ancestry. A day we can truly become self-actualized.

We have endured enough and have accepted being less than for far too long. Resetting our emotional compass to that of love and compassion for humankind is absolutely imperative. The only prerequisite should be loving ourselves first for only a bucket full of water can overflow into other streams.

We must rumble with an uncomfortable acknowledgment that the same elements of conflicts and tribalism that made the transatlantic slave trade sustainable still stifle our sense of unity and collective purpose. The world has never operated on the basis of offering a generous level of dignity and humanity to a people that don't indiscriminately apply the same level from within.

Benevolence to one who is unlike you is as African as Jollof rice and plantains. We can always go fast if we go alone. In order to go far, we must embark on the journey of reclamation, preservation and enlightenment together.

The first 400 was for us...... the next four hundred are ON US.

I love you, Cousin and can't wait to welcome you back home.

I leave you with the words of Kwame Nkrumah: *"We are not African because we were born in Africa, but because Africa was born in us."*

CHAPTER FOURTEEN

THAT BODY... THAT BODY

(Written November 2018)

"Black power, Gold Soul": An Alpha Phi Alpha Fraternity idiom as a representation of my 6 foot 5 inches tall muscular frame often appraised by many for perceived athletic prowess and not mental aptitude.

They all came lining up on the shores, some of the wealthiest men and women with acres of land in need of labor. One by one, a trail of shackles appeared with men and boys. "New slaves from the coast of West Africa!!" The auctioneer yelled. "Men from this part of the continent are known to be big, strong, and energetic! Bid with confidence!"

For some eager buyers, the inspection began as the nearly naked men lined up. The initial wiring of their brains was in active sequence, establishing visual associations and agreements that would linger for generations. "Look at those broad shoulders, those thick thighs, that butt sitting up so high, those hands... man, that's one thoroughbred!" some of them whispered.

A thoroughbred was only as good and useful as he was obedient. Dare to break away and some young girls and boys playing in the Mississippi woods may one day run into a strange fruit hanging from a tree. The kids, unfamiliar with gravity, were too naive to understand the nature of blood circulation and the inevitable pooling to the furthest appendages when in a hanging position before clotting. A pumping heart that is no more creates a reality in their minds that all "fruits" of that kind are generously endowed with an eggplant between two tree trunks of legs.

A sight of such horror not only taints their innocence but leaves a lasting imprint about the might of that eggplant. The minds of the young girls create patterns of subconscious association that eroticize features of that fruit, while the same image creates a strong fear in an adolescent boy about a vile beast that may prey on their women with the brute force of the eggplant.

(Rest in Peace, Emmett Till)

The year is 1992.

At home, Walter had the same routine with his family. The constant interplay between sports and political news his father watched religiously. Every evening, the news showed highlights of his Bulls and brought him so much joy seeing MJ defy gravity as he levitated in the air for dunks and fade-away shots. "That man is such a physical specimen!" He often heard the sportscaster bellow through the airways. The news of the day, however, always started with the vile crime of the day. Mostly mugshots of black men with dreadlocks and scruffy beards, criminals that looked just like the gangsters and thugs Walter saw in almost every movie. This evening routine continued. His brain was slowly being transformed into a binary sequence of fascinating images of Flight to indoctrinated images of Fright. Two subconscious associations of the black man. Both are "strong." One could fly and entertain, the other could cause bodily harm.

Walter went on to college to study criminal justice and joined the police force. He still enjoyed his hoops while serving his community in a noble fashion and caring for his wife and kids. One day, he received a call on the radio about a black man standing outside his car in the middle of the road. As he drove to the scene, the helicopters hovered over the man. The officer in the chopper saw the man and warned Walter as he approached. "He looks like a bad dude, man... I'd taser that THING!" Walter stepped out of his vehicle, scared of the unknown. His mind was racing. Twenty-two years of social conditioning overrides his 8 months of police training to "protect and serve." In that moment, his subconscious reigned over his being. His brain had only two conditioned points of association to draw references from and make a split decision.

22 shots later, he trembled on the radio. "Shots fired! Shots fired!... Suspect down..."

Man ... that body... that body... never got to see his daughter grow up and walk her down the wedding aisle.

(Rest in Peace, Trayvon. Rest in Peace, Mike, Rest in Peace, Alton, Rest in Peace, Keith, Rest in Peace, Philando, Rest in Peace, Amadou, Rest in Peace, Stephon Clark...Rest in Peace to the scores of slain black bodies to come)

Sigh...

Such is the dynamic of the black man; his body and the dichotomous curiosity America has always had on it. The same vibrant visuals that can elicit the most innate salivations of sexual desire can stir up intense fear of a proclivity for violence. The humanity that lies between the two extremes is often an afterthought.

To understand such a construct, one must understand the human mind as it relates to biases, agreements and the power of social associations. Our nation's first introduction to the black man was for the sole purpose of the utility of his body physically and sexually.The transatlantic slave trade itself was a man driven natural selection. Not only were the biggest and strongest black men from Africa deemed more desirable to capture, only the strongest of that pack endured and survived the journey across the ocean.

The breed of black man that made it to the shores of America created a mental imprint about our physiology based on a fallacious/inadequate sample size. So, generations of psychological conditioning and mental domestication have led to the monolithic whitewashing of our humanity and a binary coding of our nature (Physical Feat or Fright!). This is an original sin that we must all accept.

Even black boys today are being conditioned to consider their bodies as the gateway to greatness more than their minds. They grow up in a society where being able to dance, jump, run and catch are glorified equally across all races. These young men soon get a dose of harsh reality where society's "12th man" cheer and marvel about a game-winning sack on Sunday yet turn a blind eye to you slammed to the ground in handcuffs on Monday for looking "suspicious" in Las Vegas.

In her book "Blind Spot: Hidden Biases of Good People", Psychologist Mahzarin Banaji explains the concept of "Social mind bugs" that easily automates decisions and behaviors towards members of social groups or classes. In essence, our minds operate on the basis of key associations and agreements coded into our framework from the first day we set eyes on any object or person (The Black man). Understanding Implicit associations explain so much about how black men are easily deemed dangerous and never given the benefit of being "a damaged boy Nicholas who was crying out for help when he shot up the school". Our humanity is often overshadowed by the subconscious agreement about our potential nature.

Human evolution evolved significantly around adaptation influenced by analyzing our environment and an innate knack for knowing when, how, and if a reaction is necessary for our survival. Our mind's perceptions, associations, and agreements are coded over time by our culture and environment. As black men, knowing the "why" behind the level of unhealthy curiosity about our body's ability is necessary for today's America. It should influence a constant calibration on how to navigate around perceptions, stereotypes, and biases. The mental framework of our society has not evolved to a point of unbiased perspicacities.

I believe humans are social animals that are born void of hate. What hinders the permeability of our humanity and compassion for each other is the limited exposure we have to people unlike us. Many individuals with genuine love and friendship with people of different races can attest to this. Truth is that your outlook on a group of people changes the more you peel into layers of their humanity. Similar to an antivirus software flushing out malware and bugs from a hard drive, prolonged exposure extracts preconceived notions implanted subconsciously to influence human behavior towards set groups of people. At the end of the day, our human experience is quite similar to the same range of emotions, aspirations, and dreams.

Our eyes work with our brains to lie to us A LOT! Most of our thoughts and perceptions are byproducts of years of conditioning from our parents, religions, politicians, and media. If we choose to pilot our own behaviors, we must begin to challenge and seek the truth about the odious automations in our brain. Knowing your blind spot will be uncomfortable but will ultimately serve as a mirror that shows you a reflection of yourself that you may not be proud of.

So that body.... that body....

There's always more to this than meets the eye. Underneath an exterior, our society has a fascination with or is terrified about lies a lot of souls seeking validation in a sometimes unyielding world. Souls conditioned to become indestructible physical beings while the inner workings of our emotional and mental health remain unattended to.

"Who will cry for the little boy.... the little boy inside the man"
- Antwone Fisher

CHAPTER FIFTEEN

GOD, PLEASE SIT THIS ONE OUT

(Written June 2020)

Sitting at "The door of no return" in Goree Island Slave Shipping Post, Senegal in 2019 reflecting on the scores of our ancestors that sailed for South Carolina having met the 60kg body weight threshold.

I am tired....

I am constantly enraged...

I have sat alone and cried...

I am not alone...

Like many Black people across the world, the past few weeks have been filled with unhealthy amounts of cortisol being infused into my bloodstream.

My emotions have gotten the better of me some days. My impulses as turbulent as the high tides splashing against the boulder rocks of Fajara, on the coast of The Gambia. Gazing past the Atlantic Ocean horizon every morning as I pray and meditate myself into a state of calmness needed to reconstruct my mask of measured professionalism required to navigate my days.

The world's visceral reaction to the murders, racism, social injustices and oppression of Black people has caused many to grapple with a sobering dose of discomfort. A feeling of uneasiness that has for generations, manifested in Black people as pain, anger and sorrow. A menacing agitation that is now infiltrating every member of society's comfort space.

Comfortable discourse will not be in abundance here as I add a bit of nuance and address some aspects of our intersectionality.

I get triggered when I hear people invoke God and religion as an outlet for Black people to pray (AGAIN!) and *"keep hope alive"*. It invokes too many rancid thoughts about the absence of mercy throughout our history. A lot of *"where was religion when. Black people were..."* moments of painful infliction.

For certain honest conversations about Black suffering to happen... God must sit some out and allow us (humans) to face each other and confront God the brutal truths.

I'll start with the Original Sin. Yes, slavery...and side note, it's funny how slavery and supremacy is branded as White American or European, but please our fellow Arabs... pull a chair into this discussion.

The original sin when our fellow humans fell silent and unbothered as they lined Black bodies up in shackles and packed across the Atlantic Ocean, the Sahara Desert, the Red Sea, and the Mediterranean. One wrinkle of difference was the slightly higher demand for Black women in the Arab slave trade. I wonder why.

Both Christianity and Islam turned a blind eye to our hue being seen as less than. They knew our affinity to Godliness came naturally, so in-turn, scripture itself was cunningly prescribed in a way that eased their conscience into an assumption that being held in captivity was a gateway for the savage African to adopt a real religion and a true God.

The power structures sowed seeds of capitalism and global economic power on the calloused backs of Blacks never considering us worthy of just and divine valuation.

Don't take my word for it. Here's an excerpt from a letter *King Leopard II of Belgium* wrote to his colonial missionaries in 1883:

"Reverends, Fathers and Dear Compatriots: The task that is given to fulfill is very delicate and requires much tact. **You will go certainly to evangelize, but your evangelization must inspire above all Belgium interests. Your principal objective in our mission in the Congo is never to teach the niggers to know God, this they know already.** They speak and submit to a Mungu, one Nzambi, one Nzakomba, and what else I don't know. They know that to kill, to sleep with someone else's wife, to lie and to insult is bad. Have courage to admit it; **you are not going to teach them what they know already.** Your essential role is to facilitate the task of administrators and industrials, which means you will go to interpret the gospel in the way it will be the best to protect your interests in that part of the world. For these things, you have to keep watch on disinteresting our savages from the richness that is plenty [in their underground. To avoid that, they get interested in it, and make you murderous] competition and dream one day to overthrow you...."

The King Leopard sanctioned genocide in The Congo is a whole heinous topic on its own but......back to slavery for now"

"People of a lesser God.". All the echoes of our Nubian kings and queens praying to their god ISIS as they were being sold into captivity across the deserts fell on deaf ears like our Yoruba kings and queens screaming "Mercy!" to Oludumare as they were shipped away to the Americas.

Our ancestors not only had to change their names to that of their masters, learning about a new "God" was a prerequisite for survival.

Speaking of masters, allow me to uncover yet another layer of discomfort with Islam's portrayal of the Black man—specifically, the story of Bilal *(May Allah be pleased with him)*. For the life of me, I always cynically questioned why, arguably, the most revered Black man in Islamic history...had to be a slave.

The story of Bilal as told, was that of a Black man born into slavery and owned by a Meccan Arab man. He was purchased and freed from a life of torture, soon becoming the prophet's *(PBUH)* companion as an early convert to Islam. Bilal was said to have such a beautiful golden voice; his angelic call for prayers *(Athan)* became his lasting legacy as the first mu'azzin. The early activism of the prophet Muhammad (PBUH) as an abolitionist is often overshadowed because the culture all around him overwhelmingly normalized supremacy over Black people.

Now, allow me to examine that piece of history often used by religious zealots to shield away the dehumanizing symbolism behind such a portrayal of Bilal.

Hence, a Black person made a debut in the Islamic history books with his entire agency and franchise assigned to his Arab master? What if he had a voice so horrible, glass would spontaneously combust and shatter around him? What if Bilal still saw *Horus* or *Obatala* as his god and never converted to Islam? Would he be worthy of his freedom and dignity??

Thus, the fact that Black people in Arab societies face just as much racial discrimination as their brothers and sisters in the West should not be shocking. Our identity began as an inferior slave/heathen and hence even black Iraqis of today *(yes, they exist)*, face Jim-Crow-like discrimination just because of their skin color.

While our fervent embrace of the religion they introduced to our lands echoes with enthusiasm, it pains us to witness our nations grappling with the relentless grip of abject poverty. Our cherished resources—milk, honey, gold, and the promise of "seven virgins" in the hereafter—seem perpetually on layaway, while the people of the "Holy" Arab lands bask in the boundless abundance and worldly prosperity that surrounds them.

It's uncomfortable speaking about the role religion and the manipulation of God's word has played in the subjugation of Black people because it is taboo in many households. It falls under the smoldering *"things you don't question"* category, but for real change to happen, we must confront the role it has played head on.

One must assume that the "holiest" people maintaining a clear conscience as they witness transgressions against Black bodies is, in fact, a presumption that their religion itself, reinforces and creates a cloak of invisibility to protect their inherent "goodness"

As a result, history has seen Sunday church sessions in the southern part of the United States praying to the cross followed by evening burnings of the same cross as Black people were being terrorized and lynched.

History has also seen Arab Muslims insult and spit at the feet of their Black servants more often than they spat out water during *Wudu* for their five daily prayers.

Calls to prayer never led to a call to action to ease our pain and live up to God's manifestation of oneness among his children simply because mankind failed to reckon with our tolerance for evil.

Black people are damn tired of taking the high road because we, in fact, have always embodied altruistic values in our societies until we started undergoing spiritual dilution. Our faith in the higher power is unrelenting because time and time again, our fellow man has shown an indifference to our suffering. When we cry out *"But God!"...."GOD IS GOOD!"*....his grace has literally been the only spiritual safety net we have to catch our heavy weary souls from repeatedly being knocked down.

Therefore, when we are wailing and begging for our humanity to be acknowledged and respected, spare us the sermon or appeal to our "better angels".

DO NOT PRAY FOR US.....PAY ATTENTION TO OUR PAIN AND BREAKDOWN SYSTEMS THAT INFLICT THEM.

DO NOT URGE US TO PRAY TO GOD.... PAVE A WAY FOR US TO MANIFEST THE GOD IN US ALREADY.

And, if after reading this, what you get the most out of it is an "anti-religion" sentiment, consider this entreaty for a better world for Black people an utter failure. Also ask yourself if you remember. Any time in history when the world's religious centers (i.e. Mecca and Rome) were the loudest voices against the suffering of Black people.

No one can deny the good religion has done, but one must also acknowledge that it is merely a social construct/agreement that has failed to assign an irrefutable agency to Black people. A precisely packaged system designed to manipulate and influence human behavior while injecting cultural aspects that are mutually exclusive from godliness itself.

We can hope the influence leans more towards good deeds than bad ones, but our fundamental flaw as humans is also our innate tendency to turn a blind eye especially when dealing with uncomfortable and wrongful acts against marginalized groups. Man's heart and mind are corrupted through nurturing not nature.

We cannot keep invoking religion or God in matters as a key to siphon away our spiritual and emotional oasis to a state void of logic and pragmatism. God has nothing to do with how Black people have been treated over centuries now. Man has always played the role of perpetrator with cruel doses of callousness.

I believe that God will indeed be the ultimate judge in the hereafter, but moments like this in our history call for a confrontational and collective wailing of "Ya Basta!!!".

Praying hasn't worked to make the world see our blackness as an omnipotent source of melanin-rich beauty, variety, and mystery.

We can let God sit this one out and let us (humans) address our demands and desperate need for a new world order independent of religious influence.

A world that BLACK LIVES MATTER!

"Until the lion tells his side of the story, the tale of the hunt will always glorify the hunter."- African Proverb

CHAPTER SIXTEEN

THE IMMIGRANT GRIEF THAT WAS MAGA

(Written January 2017)

Stage 1: Denial and Isolation

It was the end to an emotionally taxing election season I desperately needed. I was slowly feeling isolated and disappointed about the rhetoric on all my social media networks and mainstream media. It was a new form of political banter and passion. One that was desolate, one that was divisive. I felt more distant from some friends by the day not because I had any ill feelings towards them, I just could not reconcile the dissonance in their unapologetic alignment with everything that came out of Donald Trump's mouth. Even in the absence of complete alignment, there was nothing that could have changed their mind about their vote. They had every right to exercise their agency through casting a vote for whoever they wanted. What MAGA meant to all who were in his base however, was antithetical to everything I was.

Perhaps, I was naive about the America I fell in love with and was attached to from childhood. It was the first nation I knew that jump started my active memory as a child. Moving back home at the age of seven shielded me from the elements of white supremacy and racism that were still subtly intertwined into the fabric of American society. The idea of race in itself was never binary in nature to me. The thing about growing up in a diplomatic environment is that early exposure to a diversity of cultures, languages, and nations render futile the idea of supremacy or inferiority in a child's mind. You learn to appreciate differences in others while cherishing experiences that solidify our shared human experience. Even back home in The Gambia, my version of America was always romanticized as a nation that had put the horror of its past behind and was the land of opportunity. The land that promised you a piece of that sweet American pie as long as you were willing to put in the work. It was the bargain every immigrant was willing to make. Once we "made it", to hell to our native lands we would much rather visit as "semesters" (term used to describe Gambians in the diaspora visiting home) and present a faux lifestyle than see our journey across the Atlantic as a journey of known return. A mission to retrieve all that is good in the West and bring it back home. I remember debating in my 12-grade classroom after the September 11th terrorist attack condemning the heinous attacks with so much passion because I indeed felt it was an attack on my second home. Then came Barack Obama. A glass ceiling had been shattered and nothing could have inspired me more at the time seeing a son of a Kenyan immigrant rise to be the President of the United States!!

Usher in election night 2016...my anticipated "ahhh, I told you so" moment. Donald Trump and all the divisive and opportunistic energy he spewed into the world towards people who were not White Americans was about to be rejected by the majority of people until it was not. As I sat on the couch all evening and night long, tally after tally came in with his face next to check mark. How could this be?! You have to be kidding me! Over 50 Million people said yes to that...?! The night turned into a long emotional cascade that I will never forget in my life. The experience felt like watching a loved one slowly wither and die in my presence. I had underestimated two things grossly. The tribal nature of politics "in-spite of" and the ability and propensity of over 50 million Americans to either turn an unaffected blind eye or project their vision of the nation through their ballot. Trump was the exact opposite of the life of hard work and scarce opportunity he was preaching. He simply tapped into a deep sense of bitterness over an America that was long gone to some people and, in essence, became their middle finger to the world. He spoke the language of the fear-inspired citizens even if everything he was from his privileged-laced birth was unlike the average human experience in America.

The night was rough. The next 24 hours turned into a deep sense of introspection on why I was feeling so hurt and betrayed and many questions ensued:.

- Why could I not recognize the America I knew and loved?
- Why did the outcome matter so much?
- Why did all current political news elicit unwanted emotions yet I consumed it excessively?

For the first time in my life in America at 31, I had to come to grips with the fact that my identity was perhaps, only a tolerated facet of American society and not part of the desired compilation. The country felt different from that long moment on the couch, it felt cold and most profoundly ….it felt FOREIGN. Every news cycle after that brought a level of anxiety hoping something or someone could wake us up from this nightmare and restore order. How could the most powerful nation in the world have an Electoral College system yet claim to be the benchmark for democracy? How could someone have millions more votes yet lose the election? How could people look past EVERY flaw and scandal presented by the most unqualified candidate that never had any public service experience? HOW? The world was making less sense by the day…

Stage 2: Anger

> "To be a Negro in this country and to be relatively conscious is to be in a rage almost all the time." — James A. Baldwin

One can make the argument that the election of Barack Obama turned back the hands of time in the eyes of many. It was never the version of America they envisioned. His presidency also coincided with an amplification of the open prosecution of young black men in America in a way our millennial generation had never experienced. It was hard watching the news, following social media as the rise of Trump coincided with an avalanche of hashtags and videos of injustices faced by black people in America. Situations that should have only been seen through the lens of humanity and compassion turned into political fodder and a constant assessment of whose life in America meant more. As always, I had more questions than answers.

- Where were our better angels in moments like this?

- Why did the political climate allow for such degradation of human life?

In a way that could not have been avoided, the climate of the rhetoric simply made one angry. A level of anger that came from a place of suffering. Torment that came from constant reminders that perhaps being black, a minority and/or an immigrant did not protect you from systemic oppression. The hardest part for me personally was a harsh realization that no matter how emotionally inciting elements of oppression and injustices against black people were, an unfiltered expression of my emotions was a privilege I did not have. It was the kind of pain and frustration that made me want to stand outside and scream at the top of my lungs before crumbling down to my knees in tears. There was selective outrage with a series of hashtags after each incident, but the whole world seemed to simply move on. Every morning in the mirror for me as I tied my bow-tie, was a reminder that I was a hoodie away from being labeled big, black and dangerous. Navigating the country as a young black professional teaches you that how you genuinely feel, if delivered with the rawest of emotions, invokes a level of discomfort around some white Americans that may and can work against your favor. Our culture is built to disremember or attenuate the suffering of Black people in the country. It is as taboo as ineluctable sexual exploitation of young girls in some African societies. We all know it exists but dammit why does one have to be the one to bring it up and " cause trouble." The media was complicit in such disregard in the humanity of victims and their families. Tragedies like the killings of the countless black boys and men from 2014 to 2018 became political fodder for media pundits to justify the circumstances around the incidents. What was there to debate? Seeing victims that posed no harm to society be gunned down while white domestic terrorists were dealt with such delicacy was beyond infuriating. All the neighbors said he was such a good boy that just went through some tough times but if only Trayvon had stayed in school and stopped smoking weed, he would be alive today.

I found numerous occasions during the Obama years were even white Americans who considered themselves as egalitarians could not reconcile or embrace the discomfort that came with truly empathizing with their fellow citizens. Their quandary in times of deep divide turned into a deafening silence that spoke volumes to a people that needed comfort and healing. The silence was a massive IDGAF message. The tribal order had been established and speaking up for a minority was, in essence, viewed as going against "republican values". The divisive Trump generated republican script was simply the standard to follow. BLACK LIVES MATTER!!!.. NO ALL LIVES MATTER!!.. POLICE LIVES MATTER!!! LAW AND ORDER!!

Obama himself was forced to constantly balance and channel frustrations about race relations in the country that hit home to him. How could he continue selling a vision of "Hope" and "Yes, we can" when all minorities were constantly reminded that their lives did not mean the same? Trump was very clear in the type of immigrant he saw as desirable. The one's "from Norway and Sweden" he bantered. The ones like his ex and current wife who went through the same naturalization process as black and brown people followed by her own rendition of family reunification (aka Chain Migration). What immigration was 70 years ago and what it is now is completely different. The current version poses a threat to many who read the statue of liberty poem " give me your tired, your poor, huddled masses yearning to breathe free..." in a different complexion and level of empathy.

The duality of being black and an immigrant gives you a heightened ability to pick up on subliminal messages and political rhetoric that forces one to live a life of two emotional dispositions. One that allows you vulnerability amongst kin where a collective reflection of the daunting times becomes therapeutic while your public facing self has to refrain from wincing or crying out loud.

A duality that is deeply rooted in the psyche of Black people and immigrants. Our cultures have always preached and cultivated a life of hardihood and not expressing emotions of anguish. The world could not see us in such a vulnerable state. Smile and be gentle to the world even if YOUR world was crumbling from the inside filled with fear, anxiety and unattended hurt in need of healing.

Stage 3: Bargaining

"We hold these truths to be self-evident, that all men are created equal, that they are endowed by their creator with certain unalienable rights, that among these are LIFE, LIBERTY AND THE PURSUIT OF HAPPINESS"
— Declaration of Independence, 1776

1776...what a beautiful narration of a human experience scripted by our founding fathers. Slavery in America started in 1619, meaning the canvas beautifully painted never included the face of a black man, woman or child. Our humanity was never a part of the design. The experience of a black person at the time of this nation's founding was not even worthy of conversation. The only oppression worth fighting was that of the white Americans seeking freedom from a British monarchy that infringed on the rights of settlers in America. This tidbit of history is critically important in understanding the political climate that was 2016. It is one of the issues about our American experience we still have a tough time having honest conversations about. The greatness of America for many white Americans stems from a contumacious identity that the country would be just fine as it was in 1776. It's akin to a baker choosing desired ingredients to bake a beautiful cake to completion. Said baker is then forced by society to sprinkle in some raisins and frosting onto the cake to satisfy a certain standard of inclusivity. In the baker's mind, he will forever see his creation as it was before the topping we added. There will always be a threshold of tolerability on the amount of toppings, and to some disgruntled recipients of the treat, they will still reserve the right to scoop the toppings right off.

What this great nation attempted to do from birth was extremely difficult considering the tribal nature of human beings. It is in our nature to preserve our comforts and sense of familiarity with our environment. We are not far removed from the humanity of the African being a non-factor for society to expect a complete alignment to a newly defined idea that challenges the white American identity of this nation. The history of the country not only fractured the psychological disposition of the Africans in America, but it also caused a rift in identity and solidarity within the entire black race. African people on the continent have never reconciled or fully understood the plights and horrors of their brothers and sisters that made the involuntary journey of no return. I was fortunate to attend a Historically Black University—Tennessee State University—for undergrad that forever changed my understanding and appreciation for the black experience in this country. It was history learned from my fraternity—Alpha Phi Alpha—and through the cultural nuances of the campus that added layers to my "blackness." Slavery and colonialism were the one-two punch that franchised the narration of black history through a lens that made disremembering of critical elements in our human experience a feature of the construct. The brand of the Black American experience exported back to the motherland was strategic and intentional. It was never that of Nat Turner, Ida B. Wells, Madam C. J. Walker or Paul Roberson, it was that of Shaq O'neal, Monique, M.C. Hammer, Flavor Flav, Smokie (Chris Tucker character in the movie Friday) and any character that fit the stereotypical mold intended to paint a monolithic perception. So, to many, the panache of Barack Obama was something new! A "wow, they make them like that too" kind of black excellence presentation. And even then, we reached to claim his father being Kenyan, totally disremembering the fact that he was an absentee father who CHOSE to not be a part of his son's human experience when it mattered.

The 2016 election of Donald Trump did not create a revolt against an all-inclusive America. It has always existed. The design always had a threshold built around power and agency being controlled by the majority. The moment equality made gains through the demands of society, some saw it as oppression. Politics of today can be masked around policies and ideas but our leaders, our parties, have, for the most part, made the conclusion that the nation is fighting over what version of America is most desirable. Liberalism and conservatism have indeed taken a back seat. One can actually make a certain argument that Black people dating all the way back to ancient African civilizations aligned with conservatism. Most hallmarks of being overly liberal are antithetical to the discipline-oriented African way of life.

A lot of us Black immigrants approached the country we ran to as the "shining city on the hill" with very lofty expectations. It was the immigrant mirage. We showed up at the entry ports of the nation with comfort not being a requirement for us to thrive. Our *"do whatever is necessary to make it"* mentality is only active on foreign land. We deem our nations as deserts and are sold on this idea of a land of opportunity even if the treasure chests we desperately seek after are mere mirages that keep us spinning the hamster wheel for generations. Ironically, the homelands we saw as deserts of opportunity were deemed as an oasis to many foreigners in our lands who mastered the art of creating opportunities. African immigrants are trained to be chameleons in America. A knack for adaptability that always prioritized self-preservation. So, part of my disappointment the night of the 2016 election came from a place of guilt. I had latched on to an idea presented in a foreign land to the point that my own native land was always secondary in thought.

Stage 4: Depression

> *"I've spent my whole life judging the distance between the American Dream and the American Reality."* — Bruce Springsteen

The election of 2016 changed a lot of people's perspective of America. For some, all the fear and chaos that was written on the wall had manifested with even greater intensity than anticipated. Others that hold the darkest elements of American society finally feel like they have a messiah in the oval office. The news has slowly evolved into depressing tales of how horrible one side of the political aisle is. The voices of many whose lives remain unimproved regardless of political affiliation still remain muffled. The polarity of the nation has made conversations more turgid with tribal lines being hardened even in the face of blatant hypocrisy. An overarching immigrant perspective, however, is that political climates should be the least contributing factor to unmasking the reality of living in America.

As immigrants, we take massive pride in our level of achievement in this country and Africans in particular never shy away from flaunting all the impressive degrees, houses, and riches the nation has afforded us. That rosy image of the nation has fueled an unrealistic expectation and fantasy to many Africans on the continent who in turn view that presentation as the only image of success. It has been the catalyst to the mass exodus that has ravished our continent of all the intellectual prowess it once had. Not all American dreams are in fact a delightful experience. Similar to most elements of society, outliers tend to be amplified the most when in fact, "making it" in America comes with sacrifices and trials that earn the label of a nightmare. That good ole survivorship bias.

If one is comparing the financial security of the average American, a good number of immigrants that come to America with little to no resources sign up for a life of deficit that may very well take an entire generation to gain real access to the ideal pursuits of happiness. The nation with all its perks is designed to be a Ferris wheel for many immigrants who even after attaining respectable degrees and jobs, remain below the generation wealth gap of an average white American. Working twice as hard to get half as much becomes an acceptable bargain and ethos because our reference point is that of a perceived inferior and impoverished situation back home. Our parents send us off in pursuit of higher education that come at a steep cost void of a financial support system rooted in inadequate knowledge of how money and debt work in America. Our family members back home consider entrance in the country as a gateway to instant wealth but as the Wolof saying goes, *"yelna nyu yalla sutural."* (May God always provide a blanket of discretion). In most cases, helping support family and friends back home seldom comes from a place of surplus and abundance but rather a place of empathy and obligation to adhere to our altruistic values. Some of our parents that migrate as adults tend to be less educated and are hence stuck in a gruesome hustle to support their first generation children through a life of multiple jobs and a massive accumulation of debt. It takes a generation for an immigrant family in most cases to even rightfully own the land or home they live in. Having a child that succeeds in having a prestigious high paying job through higher education still leaves the child with massive amounts of debt with little or no financial agency to jump start any form of generational wealth. The immigrant parents working tirelessly are left with little or no quality time to cultivate relationships based on instilling a sense of identity tied to our native lands. Their children therefore slowly drift away into an identity black hole where they cannot quite identify as "African American" from a cultural context but will only have their names and few traditional norms to hang their identity on. Our native land decades from now will have an entire generation of children born to African parents in the diaspora who have no emotional bond with their home countries. The mass immigration has led to an entirely lost generation without an anchor.

I never see my current "status" in America as a successful immigrant story for these reasons. Chasing after "the American dream" comes at a steep price financially and will always force you to bargain away a piece of your identity even if temporarily as it did mine. Beneath the seemingly well polished, fitted shirt and bow-tie professional lies some callous hands earned from a life of scratching and clawing through difficult situations knowing going back home empty-handed was simply not an option. No job was ever too demeaning, no course or degree was ever too daunting. Despite all the feats, none of these degrees or jobs affords me the privi-lege of not waiting to earn the next paycheck to survive or bartering my potential in search of the next opportunity. My journey started at a deficit and is still void of the greatest form of privilege in this country of ours. Choice. True liberty in America lies in an unmitigated ability to pursue one's aspirations free of constraints. It is extremely difficult to pursue "Happiness" in an environment of promissory notes being attached to every aspect of your life (home, car, education, etc.) American society describes it as "earned."

I see and meet Gambians here in America and feel a deep sense of sadness. In the parents, I see exhausted marrows who left everything that could have been back home to secure a future for their children. Void of any proper understanding of power, opportunity, and financial agency, they give the best they can offer even if only guidance and prayer to their kids in hopes that they can realize the dream vicariously through them. Their plight in the country never afforded them the privilege of adequately exposing their kids to their native lands, and no matter how successful they become, the idea of a return slowly becomes an afterthought.

My biggest fear is my daughter, Isha, growing up to see a change in tide or lack thereof and ask me why I robbed her of a real sense of identity chasing after the "American dream." I have had the privilege of experiencing the nuances of living in America and Gambia but would she? I pray she never has to work two jobs while in professional school, but would that lack of experience alone desensitize her to the plight of her parents? These are the thoughts that keep me up at night.

Rafael Cruz once said, *"Only in America can one start with nothing and achieve the American Dream."* The question immigrants in the quest for the said dream should always be: but at what cost??

Stage 5: Acceptance

"Tragedy should be realized as a source of strength. No matter what sort of difficulties, how painful the experience, if we lose hope, therein lies our true disaster." — Dalai Lama

The entire history of human civilization is filled with trials, tribulations, and check marks that force societies and cultures to collectively look in the mirror and reorient their true north. When the framers of the country wrote the American constitution beginning with *"We the People..."*, it was framed around an idea they wanted to work towards and not a status quo they chose to maintain. Progress, as a result, is cyclical in nature and never moves in a straight trajectory. Every individual irrespective of your degree of participation in this climate will be judged by history accordingly. Despite all the emotions felt and processed since that solemn Tuesday in November, I still hold true that more individuals in this country are driven by love and compassion than fear, bigotry, and hate. Politics is rooted in the ability to influence another person based on the perception of what may be in it for that individual. It's as cynical in nature in modulating human behavior as any other institution of control such as religion, militarism, etc.

We have not come far enough in our journey as people for issues of race to not be a factor in our everyday lives. Society, however, cannot continue to ignore how intertwined it is in the history of this great nation. Nations always get the leaders they deserve, and I wholeheartedly believe we deserve Donald Trump. His rise to power withstanding all and every scandal was proof that the nation had to face its demons head on for prosperity to be distributed indiscriminately. He has created a climate that makes every individual with non-inclusive ideologies comfortable to show us what they truly believe in. There is no surprise that issues such as terrorism have mutated to mean something different now that it has been perpetrated predominantly by white men with hateful ideologies. At this critical juncture in the history of our country, things may actually get worse before they get better. It will create a level of discomfort for many but present an opportunity for all citizens to fight for the soul of the country.

Working in predominantly white rural towns as a healthcare professional has exposed me to nuances of individuals that always help provide perspective. Some of these individuals have lived their entire lives only knowing what is around them. Their predominant culture is that of peace, love and a sense of community. It creates a level of comfort and familiarity that makes overwhelming assimilation of any group of people unlike them a difficult transition. In some of these corners of America where hope is scarce, people resort to living a life of fear. Our politicians and media understand this social construct and therefore utilize fear and repetitive messaging to influence behavior. America's beauty or flaws are in the eye of the beholder and every community of people has a relationship with the red, white and blue that is intrinsically unique to them. I have learned through observation that people that succumb to hateful ideology due to influence genuinely grapple with suffering kernels. On a humanistic level, no greater peace exists than that which radiates from within when confronted with another human that may be unlike you. Throughout history, we may not have been kind to each other or have drawn less advantageous cards in life, but Life, Liberty and the Pursuit of happiness is truly our true collective north.

Next year marks the 400 anniversary of when the first enslaved Africans were brought on the shores of America in 1619. I feel a sense of obligation to reflect on what the next 400 years hold for our race. Our African nations that were cradles of civilizations in 1619 have been ravaged and exploited of our natural and intellectual resources. Mama Africa has been abused by the hands of corrupt leaders and foreigners while its children still struggle to live true to the saying that "home is where your heart is."

The West has provided a new generation of financially stable Black people, but our continent is yearning for an era that all great men and women sail east. I can only speak from the perspective of an African immigrant, and it behooves me to urge us all to collectively use these trying political times to reevaluate our idea of "Babylon." I pray that when it is all said and done, my legacy will be based not on my journey and accomplishments in America but on my return back home to start sowing the seeds of a new promise. Seeking the fulfillment of a dream that my ancestors will be proud of. America can always thrive without me or any young black person of African origin. Africa, however, is desperate for the return of her lost children. We cannot complain about foreigners owning everything back home and building generational wealth when we continuously mortgage away the best of what we have to the western world. We can paint our own canvas of the African dream. Reignite our capacity to change the course of our history of being oppressed and our humanity being transactional to the world around us. This will take some sagacity and must begin with challenging the fidelity of the immigrant blueprint in America.

November 8th, 2016. What felt like a loss for me, was indeed a re-alignment of purpose and a necessary wake up call to understand the world around me. The grief I felt did not change me. It awakened me from a foggy sense of reality as I transitioned through all 5 stages of grief (denial, anger, bargaining, depression, and acceptance.) It gave me clarity in thoughts and emotions. It forced me to internalize my raw emotions to fully understand them before releasing it into the world as I seek to do now. I have educated myself about the history of humanity, race, religion and my African Identity more in the past two years than I have my entire life growing up in Gambia and America. It has made me understand the dynamics of politics I always took for granted. It has turned me into a student of politics both in America and The Gambia.

There is no such thing as a "perfect democracy" in a world that has always been a balance between the haves and the have-nots. A constant battle for ideals and a vision of nations. Agreeing to disagree should never be void of civility. A government can only be "of the people, by the people and for the people" when the people themselves are engaged in seeking the truth and exercising their franchise through voting. It's hard to present ideas one may disagree with when we constantly create information bubbles and echo chambers that feed us only one perspective. We seldom ask "why are you telling me this information?" questions making how we think and act easier to exploit and manipulate. We simply do not talk to people unlike us enough to share and create organic human experiences.

To every individual out there that felt or experienced the trauma of the election of Trump in one form or another, I pray you to heal from experience and come out a hopeful person in whatever way that makes sense to you. Vote in elections because they indeed have grave consequences. Seek to always secure a level of agency and teach your children about love and compassion for, without them, humanity cannot exist.

In the meantime, protect your peace for he/she who owns the dial to your emotions owns you.

Finding Ismail (On trials, tribulations, and new beginnings)

CHAPTER SEVENTEEN

BRAVE, AFRAID AND ALIVE

(Written May 2019)

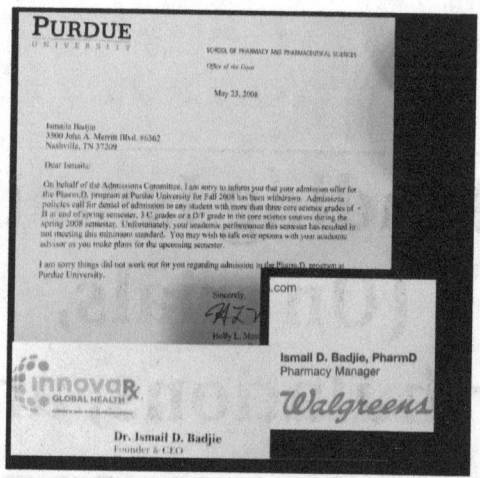

The 2008 letter from Purdue University that presented the most devastating blow in my life at the time. "If you can meet triumph and disaster and treat those two imposters just the same

I have a testimony...it doesn't make me any special, it just makes it mine

Last Semester at Tennessee State. My last semester at Tennessee State University during my undergraduate studies in Chemistry was a helluva ride. I stood a little bit taller as I strutted around campus knowing that I had made it to the finish line and most importantly, my path forward was clear as day. A few months earlier, I had visited Purdue University and fell in love with their Doctor of Pharmacy program. I chose not to apply to any other school and coasted through the interview process successfully. Well before graduation, my acceptance letter was in hand and was bound for West Lafayette, Indiana baby!! *(Ok maybe West Lafayette, Indiana only deserves one exclamation lol. Just saying. I loved the*

Purdue campus but summers in Indiana especially turned into a ghost town. The winters...well it's the midwest)

The honest truth about my undergraduate experience was that I never felt it was academically challenging. I maintained an easy 4.0 GPA in the beginning and even as I got more heavily involved with sports, quiz bowl *(Yes, at six foot five inches,, I am. a 2007 National champion in trivia, not sports. Air Captain please announce that on all the flights I get on before the proverbial "Where did you play?")* and my fraternity *(Alpha Phi Alpha)*; I made it all four years without a single C on my transcript. Was set to graduate with a 3.78 Grade Point Average and life was good.

A thing about certain habits is that you can always trace them back to your childhood. Ask any of my siblings or parents and they will tell you I was always the one to wait the night before exams to stay up all night, ace the exam and move on. I am not sure if that was an indictment on the nature of regurgitation over a display of deeper understanding in our school system but it made me take the structure for granted. I maintained excellent grades but always knew deep down I was not putting in more effort than some of my classmates. " Care-free" attitude as my dad always scorned me for.

So graduation came in 2008 and my entire family descended in Nashville for the coronation. Tennessee State had not only been good to me but our entire family. Especially the honors program under Dr. Sandra Holt (Our Dr. Mom) and late TSU President James A Hefner.

The climax had me walking on air until the rug was yanked from underneath me. The final semester transcripts that normally got released a week or two after the semester ended and was routinely an anxiety-free experience had something else in store for me.

Failure always reminds us of our immortality and shortcomings: CALCULUS II- D

The fine print on my Purdue Admission letter:

"Admission policies call for the denial of admission to any student with a D/F in a core science course during the spring 2008 semester"

I have a testimony...it doesn't make me any special, it just makes it mine.

How could it be?! No way this is happening to me! Not now! Not EVER!

That summer of 2008 tuned forlorn and gloomy quick. The grim reaper we call failure came knocking on my door and boy did he have a package to deliver.

For the first time in my life, I had to explain to people who never equated failure to me that I had dropped the ball at the most crucial point of my academic career.

Looking back at the experience, I am still ashamed of my initial reaction. It came from a sense of entitlement that was unbecoming but deeply rooted in the student I thought I was. Instead of owning up to my lack of focus and allowing comfort to creep in the last few months of school, I marched all the way up to the dean to appeal the grade and sought answers as to why the math professor was "trying to ruin my life". I blamed it on being on the road traveling with the Quiz bowl team that I captained my senior year, blamed it on any factor but the man in the mirror.

I deserved that D. Not because I struggled with math, but because I always felt like I was immune to academic shortcomings.

God knew he had to take away something so dear in my life at the time. He knew I needed that moment to change the course of my life forever. And that it did.

I think failure always reminds us of our mortality and imperfections as humans. Consistency is hard to maintain despite true natural ability in anything. So, when the moment of failure hits you like an ice cold shower, it plunges one into an immense state of depression, regret, shame and guilt that can leave a lasting impact like it did on me that summer.

Hearing *"Dang! What happened to Ish?! I thought you got into Purdue"* always felt like a knife being twisted into my rib once again. It was my first true experience with shame and left me intentionally isolated with few people who gave me a shoulder to lean on and still held their bets on my success. *(You know who you are, I will never forget).*

I have a testimony...it doesn't make me any special, it just makes it mine.

We all have moments in life when we make plans and God simply laughs right back in our face. Moments he says *"Sit down, you are not ready!...also here goes this heavy rock to put on your shoulders that you will assume will be the death of you."* Moments when you simply have to make a choice on what you will do to pick yourself back up after being knocked down.

I consider these defining moments the "hammer and chisel moment". Moments that can build a massive chip on your shoulder to use as fuel while also exposing the true mettle you're made of. That same moment could also be when you simply drop the hammer, walk away and convince yourself for the rest of your life that "it wasn't meant for you".

I still believe a part of me died that summer but the version that was born out of such a gut-wrenching and disappointing experience was one that realized that failure was more of a pitstop than a roadblock. An opportunity to not blame the world *("why me?")* but to show the world *("try me!")* what type of moxie I was made of. It built a sense of responsibility and acknowledgment of my individual role in the debacle.

Our darkest moments are designed for a level of spiritual reprogramming that can only come from within. People can offer thoughts and prayers but until deep and lonely reflection leads you to a place of peace, clarity and accountability with yourself, very few things change.

The first painful experience of failure is always for you to learn, the second one, however, is always on you because you chose not to learn. And learn I did.

I "ate bitter" that summer humbly staying in Nashville, retaking and acing the Calculus II class with the biggest chip on my shoulder. I got a job as a pharmacy technician at Walgreens, reapplied for the 2009 admission at Purdue and the rest is history.

What a difference 12 months made in retrospect. It literally changed the entire course of my life and now in hindsight. I truly believe it was exactly how God intended it to be.

I have a testimony…. it doesn't make me any special, it just makes it mine

To professor Michael Reed (wherever you are), bumping my grade to a C to get me to Purdue the summer of 2008 would have been the worst thing you could have done for me.

Thank you.

My fraternity brother once teasingly called me the "comeback kid" and to be honest, I couldn't find a better way of describing my life after the summer of 2008.

I had a relentless focus on willing all my dreams and aspirations into existence. It often made me take life too seriously (I still do sometimes). It made me incapable of being fully emotionally invested in any relationship to a fault. Most importantly, it made me see failure for the imposter that it was.

The same heat that turns carrots soft, exposes the finest of aromas in coffee beans. *(dark with no sugar, no cream please!)*

To this day, the letter of my application being rescinded in 2008 means more to me than the wall of degrees and accolades in my office. It's my constant and sober reminder to look inwards first for answers and solutions to my challenges, always bet on myself even if against all odds, and most importantly realize that I am not immune to failures.

I embrace any slight chance of failure knowing that: *"It is not the critic who counts; not the man who points out how the strong man stumbles, or where the doer of deeds could have done them better.*

The credit belongs to the man who is actually in the arena, whose face is marred by dust and sweat and blood; who strives valiantly; who errs, who comes short again and again, because there is no effort without error and shortcoming; but who does actually strive to do the deeds;

Who knows great enthusiasms, the great devotions; who spends himself in a worthy cause; who at the best knows in the end the triumph of high achievement, and who at the worst, if he fails, at least fails while daring greatly, so that his place shall never be with those cold and timid souls who neither know victory nor defeat." — Teddy Roosevelt

CODA. I remember the day like it was yesterday. The emotions were overbearing. A climax of what was a daunting four-year experience at Purdue University. My first JOB OFFER! A healthy six-figure sum amount next to my name that incited cries of *"Mama! I've made it!!"*. Not only was I about to bear the letters "DR." in front of my name, but I was also fulfilling what I believed at the time to be "the American Dream". A milestone polished with so much esteem as an African Immigrant, the pride in my parents' eyes on the day of my graduation was a gift of contentment that weighed heavier than the milestone itself. The Euphoria was numbing and the excitement intoxicating. I walked around with a *"ready for the world!"* brio to my step. Actually turned down a CVS job offer 5 months before I graduated *(boy how times have changed in the US pharmacist market!)* because I knew all along I was a "Walgreens guy." I remember having my phone interview with the Pharmacy Supervisor in Charlotte, North Carolina articulating my career plans with such precision, he could have confused my firm conviction with a slight aura of overconfidence. I was simply hungry! I was ready to torch the corporate pharmacy world with flames of excellence and potential that had been simmering for nine years! Words of wisdom such as *"excellence as a way of life"* (Dr. Sandra Holt-TSU) and *"always projecting excellence & making it to the decision-making table"* (Ms. Jackie Jimerson- Purdue) echoing in my spirit on a daily basis.

Almost a decade long of schooling after high school had honestly left me mentally exhausted, financially broke and emotionally drained.

I knew I was going to excel at my job as a Walgreens Pharmacist because my whole life up until that point prepared me for it. I had worked in the healthcare field for almost five years. Humbling tasks as minimal as restocking prescription medication products bottles on shelves in between classes at the Purdue University Pharmacy. I was also a keen student of organizational leadership. Sought out any opportunity to sharpen my abilities and emotional intelligence working with people.

Retail, on the other hand, is in my blood. A lineage of entrepreneurship through my mother and grandmother that kept evolving with every generation. Subconscious apprenticeships that began with all the long summers I spent with my mom walking 20 to 30 blocks in New York from a wholesale vendor to another watching her bargain with the fluidity of numbers and quantities without ever a calculator in most cases.

Walgreens soon became my world and being the best at what I did totally consumed me. Being a pharmacist provided a new sense of identity and pride that was an overdue transition from being a student. I hopped on "the ladder" relatively fast, too. Got my first promotion to Pharmacy Manager less than a year out of school and two years later was managing the second busiest pharmacy in the district located at the busiest intersection in the state. I was proud of my ability to take on the "trouble stores" and improve the performance of people and processes. Every opportunity was seen as a way to add "more feathers in my hat," but most importantly the relationships I was building with people were invaluable. Being granted notoriety of a "Top Performer" in the area meant something at the time and opened doors to so many opportunities the company provided which I was grateful for.

Fast forward to late 2017 when something in me changed during yet another transition to the highest volume store in the area doing over 1000 prescriptions a day located an hour away from home. What was meant to be a step up to the next level, did not feel rewarding at all. For the first time, I felt the burning discomfort of misalignment in my purpose and career aspirations. I had come to age not only as a pharmacist but as a leader at the previous store. I became confident in my abilities and felt during every single intractable hour at work that there had to be so much more I could be doing I had reached my "10,000 hours" but yet my professional fate was being dictated by the "powers-that-be"; like a pawn on a chess board. Walgreens had afforded me a valuable opportunity to grow, but deep down inside I always knew there was an expiration date to my experience. My "Potential" was in desperate need of acceleration. The two-hours a day commutes back and forth to work soon became moments of deep reflection mostly questioning my "Why":

- Why did I spend more time driving and being at work than I did bonding with my infant daughter?

- Why did I start feeling grossly under-compensated for the heavy lifting and high performance I maintained over the years?

- Why did being good at the job provide no sense of fulfillment?

I was miserable and knew a change was needed. Resentment was creeping in and I could not envision a future role or position with the company that would provide the fulfillment I craved.

So the transition was indeed the beginning of the end. I had come to understand that being good at a particular job did not translate to alignment with your sense of purpose. Another realization was also what I deemed to be the "mountain top" six years ago as a new graduate, was so unfulfilling, it manifested simply as a mirage. The money...I never saw or felt. Working as a young professional with massive student loan debt makes any "six-figure salary" a mere illusion of a pathway to "riches" and financial freedom. If anything it makes one a slave to the paycheck. Running on that hamster wheel every 14 days to have very little to keep and living in a constant state of financial anxiety.

There comes a time in one's life where our jobs become a primary source of our identity. Being a Walgreens Pharmacy Manager, a Doctor of Pharmacy from the prestigious Purdue University was my professional identity even if it failed to highlight all the different layers that resided inside of me.

I had a stronger internal desire to create something worthy of making lives of the forgotten and unattended to, better. Leveraging my experience into a new opportunity that ignited the transition from employee to employer but I was scared. I wake up still scared some days. The job at Walgreens provided a sense of esteem and stable income that created a level of comfort.

The idea of a "Successful Immigrant" in America was also becoming more and more distasteful to me. It spoke of an inferiority complex and a gross misrepresentation of the true immigrant experience . Living up the African dream became of greater importance. An unapologetic manifestation of my ancestors' wildest dreams. One that was more of a homecoming to usher a new renaissance era than it was being celebrated as a "Doctah in Americah." One that cultivated a new culture of "no, thank you" and not "yes, please" to anything that was foreign and unfavorable to our people.

My *"why"* was becoming crystal clear and the "how" could not involve my identity at Walgreens.

So I resigned. May 1st, 2019 immediately after a 7-week sabbatical from work I spent back home in The Gambia that was as therapeutic as it was an awakening process.

I have so many people I was blessed to work with and work for at Walgreens (you know who you are), from the bottom of my heart: THANK YOU. When it comes to community pharmacy practice in the US, WAG will always be second to none.

Am I still Afraid? Yes, but Brene Brown said it best: I wake up every day now feeling "Brave, Afraid and very alive."

What the next chapter holds will manifest in due time, but for the first time in my life, I feel truly in control of being the architect of my professional destiny. It comes with a steep cost and a level of discomfort and uncertainty many may not understand right now.

But my conviction is strong and unwavering. (*Master of my fate, Captain of my soul- Invictus*)

This journey I am on feels very spiritual.

So help me God.

P.S: To the late Ms. Jimerson *(May her soul rest in peace)*: when making it to the "decision-making table" becomes a daunting task, perhaps building one's own table (even if with worn-out tools) may be the epitome of choosing courage over comfort.

CHAPTER EIGHTEEN

HEART, NERVE AND SINEW... PLEASE HOLD ON

(On depression, disappointment and betrayal)

(Written January 2021)

Catharsis. There's something cathartic about laying here in my "mom's basement" at 4:30am watching the squeaky ceiling fan assume its natural order of rotation. Experiencing the same hypnotic prayer for serendipity I have maintained most nights the past 18 months. Thoughts racing and colliding like bumper cars while the world remains quiet in the night.

My sister moments after the clock struck past midnight *(on new year's eve)* turned to me while I was driving home from our customary fireworks with family *(this time in Dubai)* and asked how I felt about the new year. Only one word was clear as day: TIRED.

Like many, 2020 literally kicked my ass emotionally, mentally, financially and physically. Catching *"the vid!"* in August even feels more like an asterisk in the grand scheme of battles fought in the year.

Being in a reflective state, however, has always been my modus operandi, perhaps due to my deep affinity for seclusion. It's the reason I've always considered "New Year Resolutions" as fickle proclamations of missed opportunities to reflect, take inventory, and resolve.

How could one reserve such a powerful and conscious auto-correction tool for just one moment in the year? Every waking moment should be a resolution opportunity, but perhaps the initiative symbolism associated with *"January 1st, 20XX!"* to some may carry a significance of commitment I may be overlooking.

The numerical turnover might be the only thing that has quite changed for me in 2021. I cannot remember not feeling like a page had turned like I do right now.

There's something unique about tough moments in our life that can harden our heart in the most unassuming ways. Our armors thickened and raised up to even resist a helping hand and/or supportive shoulder to lean on. Disappearing acts of days without contact to cope and heal in isolation. Text messages not returned till days later or stoically watching incoming calls fade away to the depths of full voicemail inboxes.

Melancholic days where my tank was left completely empty (mentally and emotionally) with no "post-work" reserves for any meaningful engagement with human beings. If only they knew how laden my *"Hey, Sorry for the late response..."* was.

I could never quite label this recalcitrant trait ingrained in me early as a survival mechanism. I can be cheeky and assign it to features of a *"middle child syndrome"* or the infusion of machismo being raised in an African environment infested with Dad's ill-equipped with emotional intelligence that forces boys to numb out emotions of vulnerability.

I think psychologically I have always been the one to operate like "my cup" was bottomless, despite being completely depleted. An unrealistic assumption of being "superman". "Staying f**king hard!!" as David Goggins would scream in my social media timeline. *(I love his rah-rah energy, but he is an outlier! Even Navy Seals are not all built like him)*

People always highlight the mental health issues most founders of companies and entrepreneurs face, but what's normally missing is the "in-spite of" mentality that has to kick in. You still have to wake up prepared every single day to put out fires and get shit done, despite all the hurdles in the way. Your "A-Game" can have no days off! You don't work, you don't eat.

The very act of creating in a business can be a profound source of fulfillment, but can leave potent residues of anguish and uncertainty in every second of stillness you have. It feels as spiritual as it does lonely. Moments where only you and God are all you have to sustain the will to fight on.

It's being in the middle of an impassioned business investment pitch articulating your purpose driven vision for the company while glancing at a buzzing cell phone from rabid bill collectors.

The self-inflicted attrition felt dealing with employees seeking more pay not justifiable through their productivity on a backdrop of a payroll budget that has kept you as the forgotten soldier for months.

It's that assumption of wealth and success assigned to you in society because of a refined presentation while strutting the streets with the little financial security one had mortgaged away on a promise of a budding enterprise.

Living in The Gambia especially comes with quite the perplexing deferment of other people's woes and financial responsibilities, while balancing the paradox of a deep lack of self-awareness and ability to take stock of choices in their individual lives. Being labeled as "Privileged" can often be a vain assumption of always being able to help financially to a point that the act itself feels like a moral obligation. Our society truly has a very odd way of seeking to "redistribute wealth" with no onus for ingenuity void of a sense of entitlement.

I think I was subconsciously more vocal in my advocacy for mental health issues the past years because I was all too familiar with the challenges of maintaining my inner peace. Being able to identify that slippery transition between the extent of my intuition and the raging emergence of my anxiety. Getting the right help and finding balance is hard.

First comes the foolish shame of actually labeling what one is going through as depression or anxiety, especially in a society mostly in denial about its pervading malignancy.

Feeling like expressing your battle to a receptive, caring and listening ear will overburden them with "your problems" and assuming the pity they may offer is what you need the least. Or some that tell you *"Go-mal Yalla"*" *just pray over it"* *"God is good"*. Trust me, if everyone going through "it" can just "pray" their way out of depression, anxiety and other mental health issues into an oasis of serotonin, they would.

I do not want to downplay the importance of one's religious faith and practices in providing substantial strength and hope. However, too many times, especially in African contexts, pointing everyone's mental health issues toward a dogmatic solution can be restrictive to seeking professional help and induce more societal shame. It only calcifies more members into the "hide when you hurt" club.

Lack of access to mental health professionals due to cost, location & scarcity of culturally aligned clinicians is challenging enough as currently constituted.

Betrayal and disappointment. I faced my dreariest and loneliest days when my co-founder and friend abruptly threw in the towel without any notice in December of 2021 after almost 6 years of spending almost every moment together nurturing what I used to call "This child of ours."

I always had a sense that that day would eventually arrive. Early on, I caught glimpses of his inconsistency, but my deep love and loyalty as his brother blinded me to his personality traits that would cost us later. The company we both worked for had already severed ties with him for similar reasons that I would soon come to understand. Yet, during that time, I viewed him as the victim and steadfastly stood by his side. I was living in a sparsely furnished single-bedroom apartment in Charlotte, North Carolina, months after my divorce. Sticky notes and diagrams covered the walls, depicting my vision and master plan for the upbringing of "our child". I shielded those details from him initially, as an act of protection, knowing that he would only see the full picture if he earned my confidence.

His unwavering trust in my parenting abilities was incredibly intoxicating, and it prevented me from recognizing his lack of long-term commitment in various aspects of life, including relationships. But I believed our situation was different, that he would prove himself. And in the beginning, he did live up to that redemptive spirit, standing with me through every step of building a life for our child. I will always acknowledge the blood, sweat, and tears he poured into raising "our child", even if moments of unbridled acrimony and loss of focus would occasionally emerge, particularly during challenging times.

As the years passed, however, our dream child began to transform into a nightmarish burden, tormenting us mentally, physically, and financially. It was during this phase that things started to change

Palpable changes deep down inside, amplified whispers of *"This little light of mine..."* intuitively feeling like only one of us was truly committed to letting it shine, especially in moments of darkness.

No amount of life's experiences can truly equip you for the profound disappointment that arises when it emanates from those who are dearest to your heart. It was during that poignant moment that my initial responses were colored by anger rather than the wellspring of compassion within me.

Anger that consumed me with a tupac "hit'em up" like playback loop in my mind. *"Oh, this motherf**ker right here. F**king coward!!! Oooooh, I wish I can lay my hands on This MotherF%*^Ker right here."*

Time and time again, I had to force myself to take deep breaths, trying to steady myself amidst the overwhelming hurt, pain, and disappointment that enveloped me. At that moment, I couldn't help but feel consumed by those emotions. How could he have not mustered the spine to inform me that he wanted out and seek a respectful separation? It was clear from his repeated disappearances over the past year that he was not cut out for the challenges we faced.

To me, he was my beloved brother, and I loved him unconditionally. I knew I had no business taking on the immense task of raising "our child" based on my fiscal medulla when we started, but his constant presence provided a sense of comfort, assuring me that I wouldn't face this journey alone.

My anger arose from the profound value I placed on brotherhood and loyalty not realizing that running a company often leaves little room for a thriving fraternal spirit. I had opened myself completely to him, revealing all my vulnerabilities and flaws. I trusted him with my life. When he had to choose a middle name for his first son, he honored my father by selecting his name. He stood by my side as the best man on my wedding day. For five to seven years, wherever I was, he was right beside me.

I was angry because he alone understood the depth of my pain as I put on a brave face, proudly presenting "our child" to the world. Even amidst the crumbling circumstances, I managed to maintain a semblance of grace, recognizing my ability to remain composed.

That initial pain, anger, and disappointment surged through me, transforming into venom as I found myself trapped in this emotional turmoil, silently uttering words of frustration

"Damn! If this is a fraction of what exhausted single mothers endure, dealing with deadbeat fathers who shirk their responsibility to unconditionally love, protect, and provide for their child, I wouldn't wish it upon my worst enemy."

But, like many stages of grief, initial surges of anger ushers in some bargaining.

The emotions that washed over me in the initial days felt like an overwhelming force, crashing upon me with the weight of a ton of bricks. I found myself searching for meaning amidst the chaos, seeking truth and introspection regarding the part I played in bringing us to this point. I've always been willing to confront my reflection honestly, without reservation. While he may eventually share his perspective, here is what I know for sure:

When we embarked on this journey full-time in February of 2019, both of us grossly underestimated the mental, physical, financial, and emotional toll raising this child while drowning to keep our respective families together was going to take. The constant grind was inevitably going to break us, and it did. It was the hardest thing in our lives we had to go through, and the adversity was never going to build our character, it was going to reveal it. Evoke every last bit of our better angels in the midst of the gloomy darkness in us.

In the delicate dance of running a business with a beloved friend, there exists a precarious slope to navigate. Often, the demands of the business call for a relentless "let's go" mentality, leaving little room to acknowledge and address their yearning for a shoulder to lean on. In these morose moments, when I am prone to being snapped into a state of coldness, isolation, and compartmentalization, empathy toward those around me who also bear a responsibility to show up and get things done becomes scarce. It's a toxic trait that has cost me numerous relationships, a consequence of grappling with what I've always viewed as the curse of my ambition—the shadowy side of my being.

Regrettably, I failed to recognize that his emotional reservoir was not wired in the same way as mine, capable of continuously leaning into discomfort-laden hyper-focus and drive amidst the internal storms of deep depression and anxiety. However, in all honesty, I cannot claim to have ignored his moments of burnout, for in my perception, he had no choice but to persist. The child still needed milk! Choosing to embark on a business venture, much like raising a child, entails signing a personal contract that transcends comfort and necessitates unwavering commitment.

Having a rough day at work with customers yelling at you... guess what? The child still needs milk when you get home. Woke up feeling under the weather coughing and sneezing?, oh well.... this child of ours won't feed itself and you committed to it so.... fetch the damn milk!!

That was my disposition in the midst of our internal chaos and I know every opportunity he had to stoop down and build himself back with worn-out tools.... his new baseline was never going to be a 100% commitment.

Part of the loneliness that enveloped me in that moment stemmed from the realization that the world remained indifferent to my struggles and challenges. I understood that regardless of what I was going through, I still had to summon the birr to show up and keep pushing forward.

The weariness accumulated over the past few years gnawed at my core, making me question the longevity of the idyllic life many yearn for in their old age, the notion of sitting on a porch and finding respite from the constant grind. The concept felt transitory, much like a ephemeral mental escape from the relentless demands of life nowadays.

I remember waking at 4:00am one morning in the midst of deep grief after only managing three hours of sleep, compelled to prepare for an opportunity to speak on a webinar hosted by the Lagos Business School. The topic centered around Africa's offline and online retail channels and the profound impact of access to healthcare. However, as the webinar was about to commence, tears welled up in my eyes, overwhelming me with pent-up emotions. I was exhausted, drained. While I remained grateful for my resilient spirit, I couldn't ignore the growing callousness within my heart and the weariness that weighed upon my mind.

There I stood, mentally depleted, emotionally drained, and in complete financial disarray, awakening to an overdrawn personal account and a looming $5000 bill from the company lawyer, signaling an impending battle over the custody of "our child."

Despite it all, I splashed my sleepy face with cold water, mustered the oomph to meet my own gaze in the mirror, and tied yet another imperfect bow tie knot over a shirt and suit jacket that concealed the basketball shorts I wore. I had to show up.

Why? Because "the child" depended on me for milk. Its growth and survival hinged entirely on my shoulders. This had been my unwavering commitment ever since I signed that personal contract, choosing to upend my life and bet everything on this child of ours, regardless of the depths of the challenges we faced.

I never had the luxury of not showing up because, for me, there was never a plan B. I had to damn well succeed. My freedom relied on it.

And so, as the tears flowed, cleansing away much of the pain, they carried no trace of bitterness or guilt. I had never cheated the process of life, and sometimes God guides us down a solitary path to bring us closer to Him. Sometimes on the path of most resistance.

So in any moment of glory that may come, I will pound my chest and scream "It's HIM!!" knowing I will never be worthy of taking ownership of triumph he gifts us with.

This too was destined to pass, and indeed, it did. The waves of anger and resentment gradually dissipated from my bloodstream with each deep breath, as I embraced and accepted my new reality.

One of my closest friends Chinedu had once shared with me that placing trust in humans to always act in our best interest was a fallacy. Instead, we should trust that they will remain true to their nature, and perhaps, if fortunate, we may encounter the best version of that individual. I couldn't agree more.

Throughout life, we learn numerous lessons about the inevitability of disappointment from humans, reinforcing the notion that only God is exempt from causing such heartbreak and betrayal. Our inherent fallibility often leads us to invest faith in people, when love should be the constant foundation in any relationship. Even if that love reveals true colors that sting like bitter serums, it ultimately strengthens us. Faith belongs to God.

I firmly believe that everything we encounter, every relationship we form, and even life itself, has an expiration date. The manner in which things conclude often holds little significance. In this instance, I owe it to myself to embrace the transient chapters of my life with him in their entirety.

I am grateful for the moments of love and camaraderie we shared, particularly in the beginning. I wouldn't change anything, and I genuinely wish him the best in a life that will no longer include me.

No matter how much we may desire certain outcomes for others, not everyone will be ready, and not everyone can accompany us on our journey. The vision, akin to a moving train, must stay on course towards its true north.

The "child" was never a manifestation of HIS dream. It was always a carefully crafted vision of mine. From the very beginning, he simply boarded the bus I was driving, with the unalienable right to disembark, even if the departure lacked grace, when the twinge became unbearable. My fraternal spirit and naivety blinded me, leading me to expect a level of determination and commitment from him that simply wasn't present. This realization reinforced the analogy that humans are akin to the delicate strings within pens, where the force or constant pressure applied to bend them into a desired position correlates with the subsequent repulsive force they exert to swiftly return to their natural state. This observation holds true for the majority of individuals.

Therapy. Like many other sullen periods of my life, I found solace in seeking therapy to unpack all my $%T and turning to God for refuge. Therapy was first introduced to me in 2014 and proved to be one of the best decisions I made at that time. It allowed me to delve into the depths of my being, understanding and assigning meaning to my emotional and mental intricacies. Through therapy, I discovered various coping tools, such as CrossFit, meditation, and writing, that helped me maintain balance.

However, it's important to acknowledge that therapy was more accessible to me during the years when I had a high-paying job, excellent medical insurance, and disposable income. Affording the cost of $130 per session seemed reasonable, almost equivalent to a night out with friends. In an ideal world, mental health services would be as freely available as public parks equipped with exercise facilities. Any essential service that financial constraints can hinder access to fundamentally contradicts the universal commitment to humanity.

Interestingly, many of my coping mechanisms, which may appear structured and "legitimate" to others, actually disguise themselves as hobbies or interests. My unwavering commitment to activities such as CrossFit, boxing, running, and basketball serves as therapy for me. The discomfort induced by physical exertion allows my mind to be momentarily hijacked, providing a much-needed respite for approximately 90 minutes while simultaneously strengthening my inner resilience.

I fell in love with meditation because it gave an allowance for my mind to process, reflect, and seek stillness-induced clarity. Meditation is simply a powerful dimension for tapping into the God in you for clarity, creativity, and confirmation of purpose. Something as simple yet complex as stillness and deep breaths. *(The Box breathing technique works wonders)*

I truly believe everyone on this earth is fighting their own personal Jihad in desolation. It's why so much kindness and compassion is needed in the world. Some may believe the notion that *"Hurt people, Hurt People"* but I still ascribe hope to the contrary. I think challenging moments in life are a spiritual manifestation of self-discovery designed to equip you with tools and life lessons needed to elevate your life and that of people around you.

In the midst of my glum cloudy days were so many rays of sunshine I wish I allowed through to bask in the moment. Acute infusions of gratitude invoked by the grace of my wife, the intuitive warmth of my mother, unrelenting belief from my pops, uplifting camaraderie from my brothers, affectionate listening ear from my sisters and the pure transcendence of love from my daughter's mere presence that always felt like oxygen to drowning lungs.

Deepak Chopra in his Chapter on Dharma in his book "The Seven Laws of Success" states *"When your creative expressions match the needs of your fellow humans, the wealth spontaneously flows from the un-manifest to the manifest, from the realm of the spirit to the world of form"*

When I embarked on this journey of mine years ago, the depths of the struggles ahead of me were unclear; but I knew the path was filled with sacrifices and a purpose-driven desire to create a better world through healthcare. This is the crux of what has kept me going.

Seeing ideas that were once sticky notes that flooded the wall of my tiny one-bedroom apartment in North Carolina now transformed to a fully operational healthcare company with over 50 employees giving hope and access to thousands of people is nothing short of God manifesting his creation through me and my valuable team of founding members. Our sacrifices bonded through sweat and silent tears while holding true that God did not get us this far, just to get us this far.

On a personal note, a recommitment to valuable relationships is of absolute importance. The pressures of entrepreneurship will never change and dwelling on uncontrollable factors hinder the clarity needed to continue willing this little child of ours *(Innovarx Global Health)* into continued existence.

Being in a healthy mental and physical state is an ever swinging pendulum that requires intentionally placing efforts and coping mechanisms that shift the base of the pendulum forward and not the kinetic ball hanging by an elusive string. Like happiness, the state is an ever fugacious target that requires constant positive recalibration from within to gain daily victories.

I continue to pray the experience rids my heart of any regret, resentment, or cynicism.

I continue to pray for the ability to cope in my darkest of moments and still present the best version of myself to the world.

I continue to pray for the pith to lean in closer to my family and close friends and remain present in their lives through active love and communication.

I continue to pray for my Heart, my Nerve, and my Sinew, to PLEASE HOLD ON.

CHAPTER NINTEEN

THE WAX BETWEEN TWO LIT ENDS

(Written January 2023)

2015 New Year's Eve photo op with my mom, Haddy Ndong, and dad, Dembo Mankamang Badjie. I am, because they are.

There's a burning sense of anxiety in the stage of my life that I've entered constantly balancing the needs and expectations of the people that matter the most in my life. Society has always had a haughty approach to telling young professionals *"you must seek work-life balance"*, but that elusive harmony in an African context has a more visceral weight to it as it relates to balancing the needs of one's child and one's parents.

I am yet to put a finger on the watershed moment but turning 37 years old came with a sobering reality that my youthfulness is ever so evanescent. With my once springy and athletic knees feeling stiff and injuries, aches, and pains taking longer to recover, any night I come short of my required 7–8 hours of sleep results in an immediate fatigue-latent tax bill due the next day. This is a sobering reminder that I am not Superman anymore; Father Time is undefeated.

On a personal front, I am now a father to the most beautiful four-year-old muse *(my daughter)*, and my own mother and father are 65 and 72 years old, respectively. The two lit ends to my candle of life ablaze that I have struggled to manage and balance which lit end takes priority.

Like a candle with two lit ends, any end that gets elevated, the opposite end burns faster, and the wax melts away into the abyss.

Embedded in the slow-dripping wax is nonrenewable time, memories that should have been organically cultivated but never were.

Embedded in the wax are hopes and dreams that foolishly hinged on the audacity and irrational confidence that our time on earth *(the length of our candlestick)* was unlimited.

Embedded in that wax are the expectations on a middle-aged professional who should be dedicating his professional prime to creating and securing wealth for future generations, on the backdrop of what's often a painful realization to many that a lofty inheritance from our parents is not what is awaiting on the back end of life. The manifestation of our prowess in society, infusing them *(our parents)* with pride among their peers, has always been deemed their return on investment.

This juxtaposition, however, has been my greatest source of guilt and anxiety, knowing my candlestick wax between the two lit ends was intentionally placed above a hot stove *(my life as an entrepreneur)* that speeds up my burn rate with a phantosmia of weary nerves and sinew.

One could embody a recalcitrant flair of not ascribing to societal norms, but Black societies, unlike many, always came with an understood notion that once the children were fed, nurtured, educated, and prayed into viable members of society, an unspoken bill came due. Coming to age in your prime years *(financially)* came with a subtle but simmering expectation that it was time to reach back and pour it into the financial cauldrons of loved ones, even if you have cups of your own offspring yearning for sustenance that can transcend a generation.

It's quite perplexing when you think of the notion of "barrkeh" *(Word for blessings in Wolof)* being tied to a middle-aged child's aptness to provide financially for parents and elderly relatives. A pervasive guilt-tripping concept so embedded in our societies, people in the worst financial situations will go to any length, often void of a moral compass, to maintain the persona of the one who bought the new car for his father, of the one who buys a house for his mother, while their affairs may not be fully in order, to ensure a structured transference of wealth from generation to generation.

Despite my recognition that I have been focusing too much on one aspect of my life, represented by the unbalanced elevation of one lit end of my metaphorical candle, I still have a strong desire to do the same for my parents. At the same time, I struggle with guilt about being hypocritical in my criticism of society and the fact that my decision to take a risk and try to improve my daughter's future came at a time when I was on the verge of financial stability in my career. I hit the eject button from the highest of altitudes to hit rock bottom and attempt to slowly build back up, even if with worn-out tools. These conflicting emotions make me feel vulnerable every day.

I have been lucky as a middle child to be insulated by the provision prowess of older siblings and enjoyed the grace given by parents who understand my intentions and ambitions. They remind me constantly that their love for me was never transactional in nature nor is it tied to my ability to elevate their end of the candle. I am the child who was in school until the age of 28 so delaying gratification is as on-brand as my penchant to maintain an avoidant attachment style emotionally

Their grace however still lacks the potency to dull out the reality of the limited time left with them, nor do I take it for granted. The time that is borrowed with every single tilt of their candle *(also lit on both ends)* makes their flames burn brighter creating lasting memories while also burning faster.

The hot stove sitting beneath their candle may not be the stresses of entrepreneurship I grapple with but conditions such as diabetes, hypertension, bouts of depression, and constant worries about the safety and wellbeing of kids and grandchildren that may weigh heavy on them daily.

As the Naija slang goes *"this life no balance at all!"*

Like the wax between two lit ends, any edge of the candle that gets elevated makes the opposite end burn faster.

I hope and pray every day that God allows my parents' wax to burn slowly and to experience the full extent of my intentions, which is to not seek "blessings" through material and monetary gifts but to enjoy the fruits of their labor and know that everything they may lack today is because we, their children, are not only their investments but have the ability to become manifestations of their ancestors' wildest dreams.

The other end of my lit candle *(my daughter)* however, will always carry more weight in my calibrations because I consider her ability to survive and thrive my penultimate responsibility.

As a father, I want to be able to provide for my daughter in a way that exceeds my own experiences. I want her to have the opportunity to explore her passions and to have the financial stability to make decisions based on her own desires and goals and not from a place of desperation swinging for the fences. At the same time, I am torn between this desire and the guilt I feel about not being able to provide for my own parents in the same way.

It is a constant struggle to find a balance between these conflicting desires and expectations. I am aware that I am not alone in this struggle and that many others are facing similar challenges. However, I hope that by acknowledging and discussing these issues, we can begin to find ways to support and uplift one another as we navigate the multiplicities of work, family, and cultural expectations.

I pray she *(my daughter)* never feels the need to "repay" me in my old age but also understands the responsibility she bears to ensure the stability her grandchildren enjoy becomes something her grandfather and grandmother could have never imagined.

As I continue to navigate the medley of balancing the needs and expectations of my child, my parents, and my professional life, I am reminded that there are no easy answers or one-size-fits-all solutions.

After all, "The candle that burns twice as bright, burns half as long," so perhaps seeking to heighten luminosity in shared human experiences with the people we love has always been a worthwhile aspiration, never designed to be balanced in the first place.

I am grateful for the love and support of my family, and I am committed to finding ways to honor and care for them, while also pursuing my own dreams and aspirations.

Ultimately, it is the connections and relationships we build and nurture that give meaning and purpose to our lives, and I am determined to make the most of my time and opportunities to create meaningful and lasting bonds with those I hold dear.

*A candid moment captured of one year old Isha delivering her customary warm embrace.
" Pure Oxygen"*

E Pluribus Unum:
Out of many, one

CHAPTER TWENTY

LIFE AS A HYPHEN

(Written May 2020)

My People,

I'd like to borrow YOUR minds as a blank canvas to paint a vivid picture of my life as a hyphen.

And please pardon me in advance for any sharp contours and hues, but this quandary of mine has always shifted back and forth with dark melodies like some old rhythm and blues.

A Black man was killed in America two months ago for going for a jog in his own neighborhood in broad daylight and something dawned on me:

Being away from America and back home in The Gambia is a constant reminder of how disconnected we are from our collective trauma as Black people. See what slavery and colonialism did was to sever the nerves that reinforced the humanity of Africans all over the world.

From Juneau, Alaska to Johannesburg, South Africa—we have grown numb to each other's pain. Cries from Black boys being sold into slavery in Libya falling on deaf ears to our cousins in America, just as the slaying of Trayvon Martin not even making the nightly news in Gambia. *(There were another 100 bags of rice being donated that night.)*

Unless, like me, you swing between two nationalities, and each blow to our humanity is visceral. Living life as a hyphen between two malign worlds to the plight of Black people.

I sometimes struggled with reciting the words: *"I pledge allegiance to the flag of the United States of America, and to the republic on which it stands, one nation under God, indivisible... with liberty and justice for all."* See that was written in 1892 just 30 years removed from my tall 2 meter frame being prime property on the auction blocks of Charlestown, South Carolina.

Slave owners bellowing from the shores about features of my broad shoulders like *"Aigh nah, gatha round folks... we got some fresh ones from West Africa, see these boys and girls right here... them some thoroughbreds, now ain't he a specimen!.... Look at them hips n thighs on her, just whip'em straight... and you could ride'em ALL day long on them cotton fields"*. It's crazy how the auctioneers of back them still sound like sports commentators and scouts of today analyzing the athletic prowess of fresh meat being served up to the professional sports leagues.

Life as a hyphen

Like the movies, they have ingrained the images of King Kong swinging from tower to tower chasing the white lady in our brains to make the rest of the world TOWER over our humanity. Seeing us as savage beasts in need of taming. Such a tragic story and portrayal of the life of Kong that soon became the hill some of us died on..

Rest in peace, Emmett Till...

Some of my African people on the continent may wonder about the name of this king being emitted from me, but, you see folks, that is the tragedy of this dichotomy of my consciousness.

My life as a hyphen holds chapters of my interwoven blackness from the days I walked on campus at a university in Tennessee built for the descendants of enslaved Africans. My interminable nights during my sophomore year pledging HARD to be an ice-cold brother of Alpha Phi Alpha Fraternity came with singing soulful hymns of couth Black heroes like W.E.B Dubois and Paul Robeson, who live in the annals of Black opulence. Heroes that never made it into my social study books at Mrs. Ndow's in The Gambia. I wonder why!!

Stories told by my kindergarten teacher in New York never included ones of the great Mansa Musa…. who we all know had so much pesos, he would have laughed at the Jeff Bezos we all fawn over today. I wish I had the knowledge and bravura back then to stand up and say, *"Now wait a minute Miss Smith!, we have intellectual heroes too… have you not heard of TIMBUKTUU!"*

They preoccupied our minds to be like MIKE. Our fascination jumped from Michael Jordan to Michael Jackson as we ignored the smooth criminals that used the powers-that-be, to moonwalk away with our collective black consciousness. Dialing down the radio frequencies of our village drums so low, no hoop earrings could amplify calls to our collective awakening.

Life as a hyphen…

This paradox of a culture that passively embraces drinking concoctions of Quranic verses and tree roots for salvation, but turn around and frown upon a bottle of Hennessey or palm wine one could use as liberating libations to drown away their sorrows. A melancholic gateway that allows them to drink and dine to their ancestors' past.

Just think about it. Reliving fond memories of the days African riddles were used to sharpen our acumen, traded for our minds being played like fiddles slowly manipulating our worn out strings to a tune of rhythmless blues. Searching for all the clues once laced in the strings of our spiritual Kora tunes.

Thus, like the pair of African symbol tattoos on my rib cages, I've grown to rebel against aspects of my own *"Gambianess"* to break free from this cage of contradictions we've grown accustomed to. Iterations of a numbing folly presenting like the Madagascar COVID-19 cure. All the cognitive scars that come from a continuous belief in the things we cannot see yet ignore the palpable ones that we can see.

This is the weight I carry along every single day like a heavy shiny silver ball swinging from one reality to the next. Each making attempts at harvesting my aspirational allegiance to a fleeting sense of identity.

Perhaps the hyphen is my manifestation of the middle passage. An imaginary bridge hovering over the Atlantic ocean. An nocent road that many souls dwell at the bottom of the seas now under reconstruction as I manage the visceral blows being thrown from each realm of existence with my head bloody but unbowed.

This strange and unsettling duality I've lived with my entire life, choosing the passport of least resistance even though I pledge allegiance to THE flag…A flag….at any moment of sheer convenience.

But last week I had an out-of-body experience as I stood on the hills of Bansang where my grandfather dwelled... and heard the words *"My son, all these lands belong to him and therefore YOU"* uttered by an aunt I was meeting for the first time in my life. It resonated in a way that reminded me that this heavy hyphen of mine can, in fact, disappear.

My identity is and will always be rooted in the lands that grew the crops that fed my ancestors and their ancestors too.

Not African — American

Not Gambian — American

Just African...... No hyphen.

www.ingramcontent.com/pod-product-compliance
Lightning Source LLC
Chambersburg PA
CBHW010447010526
44118CB00021B/2533